Alternative

Shakespeare

Auditions

for Women

Simon Dunmore

A & C Black • London
Theatre Arts Books/Routledge • New York

First published 1997
A & C Black (Publishers) Limited
35 Bedford Row, London WC1R 4JH

ISBN 0–7136–4758–2

© 1997 Simon Dunmore

A CIP catalogue record for this book is
available from the British Library.

Published in the USA in 1998 by
Theatre Arts Books/Routledge
29 West 35 Street, New York, NY 10001

ISBN 0–87830–076–7

CIP catalog record available at the Library of Congress.

Printed and bound in Great Britain by
Redwood Books, Trowbridge, Wiltshire

Contents

Introduction

Shakespeare is demanded for audition a lot of the time. Unfortunately for auditioners, auditionees tend to choose from a very limited collection of characters and speeches; unfortunately for auditionees, they have to perform those well-known speeches exceptionally well to succeed amongst the incredible competition. Experienced auditioners will have already seen a brilliant Juliet, Portia (either from *Julius Caesar* or *The Merchant of Venice*) and Hermione, to mention but a few, against which we inevitably compare yours. If you use one of the well-known speeches at audition, unless you manage to hit that magic peak of performance, you are on an inevitable slope to failure.

Why do people stick to these popular speeches? I'm convinced that it's largely because they cannot face the idea of getting their heads round unfamiliar plays and characters written in obscure language. It's easier if you already have some idea of the character and play – from studying it at school, seeing a stage production or a film version. I estimate that nearly fifty per cent of *The Complete Works* are rarely performed. There is, sitting there unregarded, a great wealth of material from which the auditionee can draw. Why are they 'rarely performed'? Often because they aren't as good as the famous plays, but they do contain material which is on a par with the greatest moments in Shakespeare. Sometimes, they are 'rarely performed' because the language is especially difficult (*Love's Labour's Lost*, for instance), or because the historical knowledge required to follow the plot is too much for a modern audience (the *Henry VI* plays, for instance), or because the stories on which the plays are based are no longer part of our common culture (*Troilus and Cressida*, for instance). Shakespeare's audiences would not only have understood the jokes and topical references, but also would have had a working knowledge of their recent kings; Greek and Roman history, classical mythology, religious practices, and the Bible would all be much more familiar to them than they are to us now.

Even the well-known plays have lesser known, but not necessarily less interesting, characters in them. For instance, Hermione and Paulina from *The Winter's Tale* are very popular audition fare, but in this same delightful play are also the relatively unknown Emilia, lady-in-waiting to Hermione, and Perdita, Hermione's long-lost daughter.

Introduction

The other fundamental problem for the auditionee is length. Most people don't realise that fourteen or fifteen lines of verse is often perfectly sufficient (providing it also conforms to the other parameters mentioned in the 'Auditioning Shakespeare' chapter). Just because the famous speeches go on for twice or three times this length it doesn't mean that they mark an 'industry standard'. I suspect that Shakespeare wrote far fewer long speeches for his women because the boys who played them largely didn't have the skills to sustain such lengths of speech. I appreciate that it is difficult for women to find 'original' Shakespeare speeches, but as I hope this book proves, they are there – especially if you look at suitable dialogue and edit it to make a single speech (the Emilia speech mentioned above, for instance). Some people believe the idea of editing Shakespeare is tantamount to sacrilege. I think that this is ridiculous because there is no such thing as a definitive Shakespeare text (this is true for the vast majority of plays; most playwrights have alternative versions to what arrives in print) and also in doing an audition you are performing a mini-play separated from the whole work and it therefore will lose some of the constraints that tied it in its original context. On the other hand editing dialogue is not necessarily simply cutting out the other person's lines. It requires time, thought and trying out to see whether or not it works.

Another thorny problem is punctuation. I largely worked from five different editions of each play and in my researches to date I have not yet found any sustained section of speech which is punctuated the same way in any two given editions. I have tried to rethink the punctuation to suit the modern actor, and I have a pious hope that Shakespeare might largely have approved of what I've done – after all he was working with actors, not academics. There are a number of instances where some words vary between editions, and where there is an important alternative I have mentioned it in the notes.

Line numbering also varies, so I have chosen to number each speech from one. There are only a few instances where this is true of the speech in the play.

I have written notes on everything that might be obscure, but not following the dictates of any one academic editor. You will find I disagree with them all in a few instances. I also looked up every unfamiliar or obscure word in the *Oxford English Dictionary*, which was incredibly useful in illuminating the language. Overall I have tried to help you understand the details of each speech in order to perform it, rather than to write essays about it.

I have also included a short character description for each speech. These are meant to help kick you off in the task of reading the whole play. They are inevitably sketchy and only give the basics leading up to the moment of the speech. I cannot stress too much the fact that there is no substitute for reading and absorbing the whole play.

I have used the word 'actor' throughout this book, in spite of the fact that it's dedicated to women – after all, you don't talk about a 'doctor-ess' or a 'solicitor-ess', do you?

This book contains just fifty speeches which are rarely, if ever, used in audition. At the time of writing, I've also got another seventy up my sleeve and I know I'll be able to find more given time – you can too.

Finally, I would like to thank all those who helped me by work-shopping all these speeches before they were committed to print: Stephanie Germonpré, Sophie Ridley-Smith, Fiona Mason, Sirine Saba and Aimie Worsnop; my mother, Alison Dunmore, for supplying me with tit-bits from her decades of watching Shakespeare in performance, and my wife, Maev Alexander, for her detailed and incisive comments on everything.

Female Characters and Speeches Too Often Used for Audition

Helena (*All's Well That End's Well*)
Phoebe (*As You Like It*)
Rosalind (*As You Like It*)
Adriana (*The Comedy of Errors*)
Julia (*The Comedy of Errors*)
Luciana (*The Comedy of Errors*)
Imogen (*Cymbeline*)
Gertrude (*Hamlet*)
Joan la Pucelle (*Henry VI, part 1*)
Queen Margaret (*Henry VI, parts 1, 2 & 3*)
Lady Percy (*Henry VI, part 2*)
Queen Katherine (*Henry VIII*) – the court speeches (Act 2, Scene 4)
Portia (*Julius Caesar*)
Constance (*King John*)
Goneril (*King Lear*)
Lady Macbeth (*Macbeth*)
Isabella (*Measure For Measure*)
Portia (*The Merchant of Venice*)
Helena (*A Midsummer Night's Dream*)
Hermia (*A Midsummer Night's Dream*)
Puck (*A Midsummer Night's Dream*)
Titania (*A Midsummer Night's Dream*)
Beatrice (*Much Ado About Nothing*)
Emilia (*Othello*) – the 'Yes, a dozen...' speech (Act 4, Scene 3)
Marina (*Pericles*)
Lady Anne (*Richard III*) – the funeral scene speeches (Act 1, Scene 2)
Juliet (*Romeo and Juliet*)
The Nurse (*Romeo and Juliet*)
Katherine (*The Taming of The Shrew*)
Olivia (*Twelfth Night*)
Viola (*Twelfth Night*)
The Jailer's Daughter (*The Two Noble Kinsmen*)
Hermione (*The Winter's Tale*)

I have cited specific scenes / speeches against a character, where there is material elsewhere for that character which is not too often used. This list is by no means exhaustive – other auditioners will have other characters and speeches they've seen too often.

Shakespeare – The Actors' Writer

Shakespeare, and others, wrote for a theatre that had minimal sets and an audience that did not sit quietly watching – they reacted like a modern football crowd. (Conditions that they are attempting to recreate at *Shakespeare's Globe* theatre on London's South Bank.) He had no lighting beyond available daylight and the occasional flare or candle, no sophisticated special effects and no modern sound systems. There was some live music and the occasional drum, trumpet, cornet, and so on, but all the emphasis was on the power of the excitingly spoken word. And that's what Shakespeare gave actors: a brilliant vehicle, his words, that can really help the auditioning actor – also without sets, lighting, and so on. He also had incredible insights into how people 'tick', in a way that wasn't really generally understood until about a hundred years ago – famously through Freud and in the acting world through Stanislavski. Of course other writers of his period, and after, also 'dug inside how people work', but not so much for the theatre. There is a story about a man after seeing his first Shakespeare production: 'Hey, this guy knew about Freud three-hundred years before Freud.'

Shakespeare the Man

We have a number of tantalising facts about the real person, but not enough to write a definitive biography. One thing we are sure of is that he managed to make a good living out of writing and staging plays – he had a commercial eye for what would attract audiences. He looked for popular subjects and tried to avoid controversy by writing plays set either remote in time and / or set in other countries. (Only *The Merry Wives of Windsor* is set overtly in the Elizabethan here-and-now, and that doesn't contain any kings, princes and so on – people who if offended could be highly dangerous.) He didn't write contemporary satires to attract audiences – unlike Ben Jonson, his friend and nearest rival as a playwright – and he seems to have avoided any trouble with the authorities, unlike Jonson who spent time in prison. I think that because he didn't have any political axe to grind, he concentrated on the people in his plays rather than contemporary politics. Issues relevant to an Elizabethan are largely only of interest to an historian of subsequent generations. I believe Shakespeare's apolitical approach and his concentration on the personalities involved helped to ensure his immortality. I'm not saying that he didn't write about politics at all, his plays are full of examples; but he didn't take sides. For example, though there is a lot in *The Merchant of Venice* which is anti-Semitic (shockingly so to a modern audience), Shylock, the money-lender, has some wonderfully sympathetic moments including this (from Act 3, Scene 1): 'I am a Jew. Hath not a Jew eyes? Hath not a Jew hands, organs, dimensions, senses, affections, passions? Fed with the same food, hurt with the same weapons, subject to the same diseases, healed by the same means, warmed and cooled by the same winter and summer as a Christian is? If you prick us, do we not bleed? If you tickle us, do we not laugh? If you poison us, do we not die? And if you wrong us, shall we not revenge?'

As a playwright Shakespeare wasn't working in isolation, he was a member of several acting companies, principally the *Chamberlain's Men* (later known as the *King's Men*). I'd like to suggest that *The Complete Works* came not just from one man but through the energy and ideas generated by groups of people working closely together. A man called 'Shakespeare' may have written a lot of the words, but he must have used their experiences to inspire much of the detail. And, knowing actors, I'm sure they had plenty of their own suggestions – good and bad – that were incorporated into the scripts we now have. This is the cradle, the sustenance and encouragement that nurtured the 'genius' we label 'Shakespeare'. Over half a century later another genius, Sir Isaac Newton, the scientist, wrote, 'If I have seen further it is by standing on the shoulders of giants.' I suggest the same could be said of Shakespeare and his plays.

Elizabethan England

Not only was he almost certainly helped by his actors, but also by the comparatively stable political climate of the first Elizabethan age. As often happens in his history plays, the threat of invasion (and vice-versa) was common in the reigns of Queen Elizabeth I's predecessors. This required armies and ships, which were a huge drain on the national exchequer and when she ascended the throne England was not very well off. Her immediate predecessor (and elder sister), Mary, was a Catholic; Elizabeth, a Protestant, was a ripe target for Catholic France and Spain – England's principal rivals. There were also a number of people in England who thought that Protestantism had gone too far and would have welcomed an invasion. However, the two continental countries were at loggerheads and ignored

England until the Spanish Armada in 1588, thirty years after Elizabeth had ascended the throne. In the interim the English ships had been used for lucrative trade and exploration, thus building a strong economy, strong enough to fund the soldiers and sailors for the defeat of the potential invaders by the time of the Armada; and strong enough to support the social welfare of the nation. 'We were just in a financial position to afford Shakespeare at the moment when he presented himself.' (J. M. Keynes, Economist)

Elizabethan English

Elizabeth was the most extraordinary woman, highly intelligent and literate, and she used her power for the sake of the people, not just for her own ends, as most previous monarchs had done. She created a nation, with the help of some brilliant chief ministers, which had 'a zest and an energy and a love of life that had hardly been known before' (Anthony Burgess). This 'feel-good' factor, that modern politicians yearn for, created a new pride in the English language. Previously, Latin had held sway through the church, over the bulk of printed literature and throughout the limited education provision that existed then. People spoke to each other in various English dialects, but the use of the language in written form was extremely limited. Anything important was written in Latin, with its very strict rules of grammar and spelling – but there were virtually no official rules of spelling and grammar for English. Witness, the varying spellings that we have of Shakespeare's own name: 'Shaxpere', 'Shogspar', 'Choxper', and so on. These arise because each writer of the name (or any word) would write down the sound of what he'd heard as he would like to spell it. The written English of that time was 'not fixed and elegant and controlled by academics' (Anthony Burgess) – it was a language ripe for exploration and development, as the sailors were doing with material goods in the new world.

All this lack of regulation means that it is very common for Shakespeare's characters to commit what we would now consider to be grammatical howlers, for instance plural subjects combined with singular verbs and seemingly non-sensical changes in tense. However, he was writing down (in elevated form) how people speak and these 'howlers' often reflect the characters' state of mind.

The Plots of Shakespeare's Plays

The commercial playwright had to write plays that he could be reasonably sure would attract an audience and took his plots from existing sources that would be generally known and appeal to a paying public. Early works included *The Comedy of Errors*, a free adaptation of a well known Roman comedy of confused identity and *Titus Andronicus*, a sex and sadism horror that would put today's film censors into a complete spin. The three parts of *Henry VI* and *Richard III* are based on historical accounts of one of England's most troubled times which were finally resolved by the acquisition of the throne by Henry VII, grandfather of the ever-popular Queen Elizabeth I – an event which happens at the end of *Richard III*. A modern equivalent might be dramatically to chart Winston Churchill's life from his 'wilderness years' (forced out of politics) to the triumph of the surrender of Nazi Germany.

Another aspect of this commercialism was the 'megabucks' that could be made by special one-off performances for rich patrons. For example, *Macbeth* was probably written for performance before King James I (Elizabeth I's successor). Banquo, one of Macbeth's victims in the play, was reputedly an ancestor of James; Shakespeare radically altered the available historical record to ensure that the King was not offended and included references to witchcraft, breast-feeding and tobacco – subjects very close to James' heart.

Some Significant Speeches in Shakespeare's Plays

It's not just the plots that Shakespeare adapted from known sources, he even adapted other people's words. For example in the court scene of *Henry VIII* (Act 2, Scene 4), Queen Katherine's wonderful speech beginning 'Sir, I desire you do me right and justice...' is an almost direct copy of what she actually said, according to the historical record. Enobarbus' famous speech 'The barge she sat in...' in *Antony and Cleopatra* (Act 2, Scene 2) is very close to a translation from Plutarch's *Life of Antonius*.

Shakespeare's Texts

Four hundred years on, it is difficult to be sure that every word in a Shakespeare play is exactly as he first wrote it. The problems with his play-texts begin with the fact that then there was no such thing as a law of copyright. That wasn't to arrive for another hundred years. Once a play was in print, anyone could simply copy and sell their own version with no royalties going to the original writer. Worse than this, once in print, other companies could put on their own productions in competition. So Shakespeare himself had very few of his own plays printed. About five years after Shakespeare's death, two of his actors John Heminge and Henry Condell put together what scripts they had into print: *The First Folio*, the first – nearly – *Complete Works*.

Amongst their sources were:

(a) Some of the original hand-written cue-scripts (just the individual actor's lines and his cue lines).

(b) Some previously published editions of individual plays, the 'Quarto' editions. ('Quarto' literally means the size of a piece of paper created by folding a whole sheet twice so as to form four leaves or eight pages. 'Folio' means folding that sheet once to make two leaves or four pages.)

(c) The memories of surviving actors.

None of these can be sworn to being entirely accurate because:

(a) Even the best handwriting of the time is sometimes hard to decipher. (We don't have any texts in Shakespeare's own hand.)

(b) Printing in his time wasn't entirely accurate. Think of having to place every letter, space and punctuation mark – each in the form of an individually-moulded piece of lead – into a frame that then went onto the presses. *The Complete Works* (with *The Two Noble Kinsmen*, which is not always included) total about 950,000 words, which is over five million characters; i.e. an average of roughly 25,000 words and 137,000 characters per play. Also some of the Quarto editions were printed from manuscripts written down during performances by people trying to 'pirate' the plays (often known as 'Bad Quartos').

(c) Sometimes actors have very accurate memories for lines they've said on stage; sometimes they improve on what the playwright actually wrote down; and sometimes, the lesser ones make a hash of the playwright's intentions.

Shakespeare probably didn't write every word anyway. There are at least four other writers who almost certainly contributed to what we now know as *The Complete Works*. It also seems to me likely given the circumstances in which Shakespeare wrote – for a specific company of actors – that they might well each have had their individual 'say' in the details of what their characters said and some of their ideas incorporated.

Further confusion is added by the fact that just one copy of a Quarto or Folio edition would be printed, proof-read and corrected, then a second copy would be printed, proof-read and corrected, and so on. Nobody knows whether these time-consuming processes were undertaken for every individual copy, but (to date) nobody has yet found two identical copies of *The First Folio* from the roughly 230 that survive.

There has been such a mass of intellectual detective work trying to establish a perfect version of the text that I believe it is easy to get the impression of a super-human being whose works must be approached with over-weening reverence. Shakespeare was a human being like the rest of us. He was possessed of a brilliant feel for the use of language and how people really feel deep down inside.

I do not say all this to try to bring Shakespeare down from his pedestal; I say it to humanise a man whom others have deified. I don't deny that a nation needs her heroes, but I think that England has elevated 'The Bard' overmuch. True he was part of an innovative (even revolutionary) group that has rarely been matched for its degree of positive development. But, in order to bring life back to his works, nearly four centuries after his death, we have to feel for him – as a jobbing craftsman needing to sell his wares to make a living. We need to make his creations have real life, rather than being some too often regurgitated ceremony that sounds stale.

Finally, I have to add that without the presiding genius and humanity of Elizabeth I we almost certainly wouldn't have known anything of him at all. Periods of great art arise when the prevailing governments are prepared to invest in their nation's culture.

The Lives and Times of Shakespeare's People

It is obvious to say that life was very different for people in Shakespeare's time. To recreate his characters it is important to have some insight into how 'different'.

Birth and Death

It was quite normal for a baby and / or the mother to die at or soon after birth. It is really only since the second world war that such deaths have become rare in Western society. Even if the child survived the crucial early period, many only managed it to their teens. A working class family would aim to breed as many children as possible as workers to help the family's meagre fortunes. Many women, even if they survived the multiple births, were dead of exhaustion by their thirties. The men had the hazard of the frequent wars. Medicine was very rudimentary – if not grotesquely inaccurate – and too expensive for all but the aristocracy, so disease and malnutrition meant that people, on average, lived about forty years. You were considered grown up by about the age of fourteen and old by your mid-thirties.

The aristocracy were better fed and had access to what medicine was available, but their chances in childbirth weren't much better and overall life-expectancy wasn't that much greater. (Though, the real Richard III's mother managed to live until she was eighty.)

Contraception was available (in fact the first evidence of its use dates back nearly four thousand years), but was generally only used for illicit sex. (A pig's bladder for the men and half a lemon for the women, for instance.)

Marriage

In Elizabethan England the age of consent was twelve and it was common for women to give birth in their early teens. Lady Capulet says to her fourteen year old daughter Juliet:

> Well, think of marriage now. Younger than you
> Here in Verona, ladies of esteem,
> Are made already mothers. By my count
> I was your mother much upon these years
> That you are now a maid. (*Romeo and Juliet*, Act 1, Scene 3)

Prior to this period dynastic marriages often took place at even younger ages – for example, the real Richard II's wife, Isabel, was seven when she married him. This occurred when important families wanted to expand their power and possessions by alliance through marriage – equivalent to modern corporate mergers. The marriage partners often had no say in the course of events designed for them.

Democracy

Although the idea of running England through a democratic system started to evolve some three hundred years before Shakespeare, the monarch was still very much in charge – if he or she was strong and ruthless enough. Parliament consisted of the nobility, senior church-men and representatives of the general population. However, it wasn't a democracy as we would now think of it; more a collection of power groupings who used military muscle to get their way. The nobility had the threat of their private armies; the church (prior to Henry VIII's break with the Roman Catholic church) could threaten to call on military aid from fellow catholic countries. There were also representatives from each town big enough and two knights from each shire (or county) – but these people couldn't call on armies to back up a point, so they had very little actual influence on major issues. Right up to the latter half of the nineteenth century only a small proportion of the male population of the 'civilised' world was allowed to vote; a certain level of wealth and / or literacy being the usual qualification. In Great Britain women had to wait for the twentieth century to be allowed to vote.

Law and Order

There was no national police force and the legal system was fairly arbitrary – generally, favouring the rich. It was comparatively easy to commit and cover up crimes, if you were clever about it. It was also fairly easy to be arrested for something you hadn't done if you were vulnerable and someone with the necessary finances wanted you imprisoned.

Travel and Communications

The only forms of land travel were either on foot or using a four-footed animal, the horse being much the fastest. The latter were too expensive for the ordinary man and consequently the majority of ordinary people would never leave their home town or village. Even those who became soldiers would travel by foot. All this meant that transmitting messages and moving armies took an inordinate amount of time.

Even someone with exceptionally fast horses could only travel at an average of about twenty miles an hour, so it would take at least a day to travel from London to York, for instance. If you did ride this far, only stopping to change to fresh horses, you'd be utterly wrecked by the time you got there.

Taxation

In medieval times the monarch really only needed taxes to pay for wars, his general living expenses came from income from property he owned. By Shakespeare's time the tax system was more extensive in order also to pay for the ever expanding machinery of government. The ruling powers would, arbitrarily, invent a tax to cover an immediate financial problem. The concept of 'fairness' in taxation doesn't really occur until the late eighteenth century and 'income tax' was first introduced in 1799.

The Church

The church had enormous influence on people's lives, the power of the concept of 'God' was all prevailing – with no alternative view on the way the world worked. All but the most widely read would not challenge the idea that in order to have a good 'after life', you'd have to conform to the church's dictates in this life. Science was only just beginning to question some of the church's teachings – coincidentally, a prime-mover of this questioning, Galileo Galilei, was born in the same year as Shakespeare (1564), though it wasn't until the year of Shakespeare's death (1616) that he was taken to task by the church authorities for his revolutionary ideas.

It is also worth mentioning that the other most wonderful publication during the reign of King James I was the English language version of the Bible, which was still in common use until very recently.

Education

Education was just beginning to expand. It wasn't just the wealthy who could learn to read and write. Free schools were opening up, paid for by more enlightened boroughs and open to children of worthy local citizens, i.e. the elite of the middle-classes. The lessons consisted mostly of Latin studies, the language in which most of the limited printed matter of that time was issued; and a drilling in of their duties toward God, the sovereign and 'all others in their degree'. The poor had to wait until the late nineteenth century for the right to universal education.

Sanitation

Even in London there was no such thing as main drainage systems; sewage was simply dumped in the street – to be carried away by the rains, when they happened. Plague was a regular occurrence and public places such as theatres were closed when it struck to prevent further infection. Country areas, like Shakespeare's Stratford, smelt sweeter and people's health was generally better than in cramped and stinking London.

Light and Heat

Burning what you could acquire was the only source of these basics; there were no national fuel grids of any kind.

Primitive but survivable, England was just moving from an aristo-cratically run society to one where even the lowliest individual was beginning to matter – only thirty-three years after Shakespeare died, the English executed their king and parliament ruled without an absolute monarch for eleven years.

Within the confines of this book I can only briefly evoke a few basic aspects of life in Shakespeare's time. A character's life is not just battles and loves, won and lost; it is also the ordinary, everyday aspects that the dramatist misses out because they are not dramatic and don't serve the life of the play. In order to bring those characters to life you should find out as much as you can about how their lives were lived outside the action of the play.

Auditioning Shakespeare

Shakespeare acting – at root – is not different from 'modern' acting. Where it is different is in that his language uses words, phrases and expressions we no longer use; and (more importantly) the circumstances are invariably far away from our direct experience. It is your job (whether aspiring or professional) to steep yourself in the culture that influenced his plays if you are to perform pieces from them.

Many actors argue that doing an audition speech is a desperately artificial way of having their worth assessed. I would tend to agree but, however much you may hate them, you will periodically have to do them. Of course it's an artificial situation, but isn't acting about making artifice seem real? There are ways of making them work – think of Bob Hoskins in *Who Framed Roger Rabbit* and Steve Martin in *Dead Men Don't Wear Plaid*, both acting with beings who weren't really there.

I have 'road-tested' all the speeches contained in this book; it is now your job to research and rehearse those of your choice. You also need to prepare yourself for the varying circumstances you could be asked to perform them in. Think of an audition speech as a 'mini-play'; you are going to present a 'mini-production' of it.

Preparations

There are a number of things to consider before you start rehearsing your speeches:

Iambic Pentameters

Apart from the unfamiliar words, phrases and expressions, this verse form (popular in Shakespeare's time) is off-putting – on the page – to many people. I think it's a good idea to think of it not as poetry, but as verbal music: that is words and phraseology that people use when they have a real need to express themselves or 'touch the souls of others'. A good playwright not only writes good stories and creates credible characters, but also writes in language that will 'grab' an audience – language that has a music of its own. Shakespeare was a master of verbal music, along with Samuel Beckett, Harold Pinter, Sam Shepard, Edward Albee, David Mamet, Arthur Miller, Alan Ayckbourn, and too many more to mention. It is not so much plots that make great playwrights, it is their use of language.

11

Rhymes

Some of the verse rhymes, which can sound terribly forced and unnatural if you emphasise the rhyming words too much. You can't avoid the rhyme, but it's important to make it sound natural and not forced (as poetry is often read).

-èd

All the accent on the 'e' means is that you pronounce the 'ed' where you normally wouldn't. For example: we'd normally pronounce 'imagined' not sounding the 'e'; but if it's written 'imaginèd', you pronounce it 'imagin-ed'. Some editions (mostly older ones) miss out the 'e' if it is not to be pronounced and insert an apostrophe instead and leave it there, unaccented, if it should be sounded.

i', th', and so on

Some people balk at these foreshortened words. All this means is that you pronounce them literally as written. Listen to yourself and others in normal conversation to observe how many letters we miss out.

Making Sense

As you start out on a speech look at the sense, ignore the verse. Look for the full stops, even if they arrive halfway through a line. Then, look at each clause within that sentence; then put that whole sentence together to make the sense of the whole of it. Then, start to put the sense of the whole speech together – still ignoring the verse.

Finally, look at what words begin and end a line of verse, they may have a significance that you haven't previously recognised. After you've been through all the processes of finding and becoming the character, the positioning of these words may add to your understanding of her.

'The multitudinous seas incarnadine' (*Macbeth*, Act 2, Scene 2)

In his musical on the life of William Blake, *Tyger*, Adrian Mitchell had Shakespeare appear as a cowboy, or 'pen-slinger': 'I can drop 'em with one line'. It's that turn of phrase (that has now degraded into the 'sound-bite') that makes Shakespeare's language so exciting. It is your job also to make it 'real' for the character – don't sing it, believe it.

Preconceptions

With the famous characters, forget any preconceived notions you may have, e.g. Hamlet is 'mad', Juliet is 'wet', and so on. Part of Shakespeare's insight is that he created (mostly) very real people who may primarily exhibit one aspect of human behaviour through the circumstances of the play; but, as in life, there's far more to them than that. Think how often you meet someone new, get the chance to get to know them and find that there's 'far more than meets the eye'. The aim of this book is to steer people away from these too well-known characters, but the same kind of preconception can take over and dominate the performance. For instance, Dionyza (from *Pericles*) seems like a classic 'baddie', but in her eyes she has good reasons for wanting rid of Marina – fundamentally she wants the world better for her own daughter; a good maternal instinct. It's her means that seem extreme to us, but in Shakespeare's time she would have had a very good chance of getting away with Marina's murder – life was cheap.

Selecting Speeches

Read through the speeches in this book and see which ones create sparks for you, without necessarily fully understanding the content. (Largely, ignore the notes and character description at first, these come later.) If the 'music' of the words feels good then you are over halfway towards finding a speech suitable for you. It can also be a good idea to read them – carefully – out loud, without any sense of 'acting' them. Then read the 'Character Descriptions' to see if the characters are appropriate to you (age, type, and so on) and assess whether it's worth going further.

Don't be tempted simply to go for ones with the most spectacular emotions – auditioners want to see real feelings not flashy melodrama.

Length

An audition speech doesn't need to be more than about two minutes long and can be shorter, which can feel too short whilst you are doing it. Interestingly, Shakespeare speeches often work better when they're even shorter; I think that it may be something to do with the fact that he packs so much into his characters – a few of his words can speak such volumes. Many people think that they're not doing enough with fourteen or fifteen lines of verse – which will probably last only about one and a half minutes. Providing the speech has a complete journey to it, it doesn't matter if it's this short. On the other hand, you can lose your audience if you go on for forty lines. You may argue that there is no way you can show enough of your skills as an actor in such a short time. True, you can't show everything, but you can give a very good indication of your potential – like a good television commercial.

How Many?

For too many people the 'Shakespeare' is the speech they least want to do, and they strain even to get the minimum (of one) together. I think this is very silly. The best results I've seen have come from people who've worked on four or five – and even more. Especially if you are new to acting in his language (as opposed to just reading it), working on several speeches at once can give you a much broader insight into his world. And if you begin to fall out of love with one or two of them, you've got the others to fall back on. If you only start with one, you've got to start all over again if you become dissatisfied with it.

Verse or Prose

Some auditioners insist that you present verse speeches, so it is important to have at least one in your repertoire.

Read the Whole Play

Next, read the whole play (slowly and carefully), read a few commentaries and if possible talk about the play and its people with someone who knows it. It can be helpful to read a summary first and then read the play, but bear in mind that these merely sum up the major plot and what happens to the people, without giving much psychological insight.

When a play is completely new to me, I find it helpful to copy out the cast list and write notes about each character as they appear. Obviously this takes time, but it's extremely helpful to the process of getting under the skins of the characters.

On the other hand, don't spend hours flicking backwards and forwards to the footnotes to try to understand every line. A general sense of the people and events is all that's needed at this stage (and how your character fits in). It's important to get some idea of the flow of the whole thing – too much stopping and starting can make you lose any idea of the whole.

It is not sufficient just to read the scene a chosen speech is from – you won't gain proper insight into where your character is coming from.

The Immediate Context

When you've got hold of who your 'person' is, build up the stimuli that affect her: the other people (present and / or influential), the circumstances (place, time, and so on) – as well as the immediate provocation for the speech.

The Details

One of the fundamental keys to good acting is the degree of detail with which you imagine the above. For example, if your character is in a castle, it's not any old castle, it's somebody's home – maybe your character's own. Look at pictures and, if possible, visit castles that are preserved as they were lived in (ruins will only give a partial impression). Try to absorb the details of what it might have been like to live in one. (Touch bare stone walls, that'll give you a very strong feel for medieval living.) In short, find out (and imagine if you can't find out) as much as you can about the 'ordinary' bits of the life your character might have led that are not mentioned in the play.

The Clothes

A supremely important 'detail' is the clothes your character(s) would wear. I'm not suggesting that you dress in period clothes, but to imagine the feel of wearing them, or whatever is appropriate to the period and circumstances of the speech. One of the principal omissions I see is the sense of wearing a skirt that goes right down to the ankle. It is only in the last hundred years that skirt-lengths have started to rise above that level. Different clothes, including shoes, make you move in different ways.

The Notes

Begin to understand the details of the words and phrases of the speech through using my notes and those from a good edition of the complete play. (See my Bibliography at the end of this book for suggestions on this.) Write out your own translation into modern English if you find that useful, but don't become wedded to that translation, you'll find it hard to go back to the original. It's probably best to write it out and then throw it away, so you get a better idea of the sense without becoming fixed on specific modern words and phrases.

The notes attached to some established editions can confuse with cross-references irrelevant to acting. They may be written 'about' the character, rather than for the person acting her. On the other hand, the notes in some exam text 'note' books can tend to over-simplify.

Research

When there are real people involved it can be useful to research what we know about them. However, Shakespeare had a rather 'tabloid' attitude to the truth. The 'history plays' are based on real historical events (*Henry VIII* ends only thirty one years before Shakespeare's birth), but, like many other playwrights since, he doesn't always follow historical facts as we now understand them. Sometimes this is because the then limited historical research was inaccurate; sometimes it is because reality doesn't necessarily make good drama (this is common to all drama); sometimes (especially in *Henry VIII*) he couldn't risk the wrath of current sensibilities; and possibly sometimes he was writing too fast to research properly or he was simply lazy. Do research, but don't let inaccuracies confuse you: take what you can from history but the information gleaned from the play must finally be the deciding factor.

Learning the Lines

Don't sit down and learn the lines parrot fashion. In all this research into the background detail, keep going back to the play, your character and her speech, to check that what you've found out (and used your imagination to create) still fits with what's in the text. You will find those lines simply start 'going in' the more you understand them and the circumstances of them being spoken.

If you find that parts will not 'go in' by this process of study and absorption, then it is almost certain that you haven't fully understood what they mean.

Don't Generalise!

Because it's a speech too may people tend to generalise, and it all comes out sounding the same. In life very few people anticipate speaking at such length except in specific circumstances. You should think of it as a series of connected thoughts and ideas – the circumstances stimulate the first thought to come out as words, then another arrives and needs to be spoken, and another, and so on. Usually, at the beginning, you should convey the impression you don't know what you are going to say at the end.

Soliloquies

Shakespeare is famous for these and some people think that they should always be addressed to the audience. With obvious exceptions (the Chorus and some of the clowns, for instance), I believe they are the characters talking to themselves – 'for' the audience. When we talk to ourselves in life we keep it private and mutter. In acting we have to communicate to an audience – this is one of the fundamental differences between the 'being' process above and acting. You've got to go through the first stage of 'being' before you can go on to 'act' your speech. Don't try to prepare the other way round.

It's useful to think of soliloquies as the character thinking aloud in order to try to organise her jumbled thoughts.

Difficult to Say Words and Phrases

If you find yourself consistently tripping over a word or phrase, try saying it in isolation – with a lot of over-articulation. Do this slowly and carefully lots of times and you'll find it'll become second nature to you.

Obscure Words and Phrases

I am still amazed by the fact that if the actor understands these – in her soul – the general sense will communicate to whatever audience is watching, and they don't need extra demonstration. This 'understanding' is not simply a mental process, it is a feeling for what the word or phrase means so that it becomes a totally natural thing to say in the circumstances.

First Steps

When you think that you know and understand what your character (or 'person') is talking about and understand their circumstances, start saying the lines out loud – aiming to talk to whomsoever is or are the recipients of the words. Don't think of it as acting; you are slowly beginning to become the 'person' who is saying those words – through the speaking of them combined with all your thinking and research. Take a line or two at a time, and go back over each small section several times until you begin to feel you are emotionally connecting. You should begin to see the circumstances really happening in your imagination. One (pre-drama school) student I taught was really getting inside a Richard II speech; suddenly he stopped and said, 'I can see those f****** horses!' I shouted, 'Keep going!', and when he finished we talked about his experience. The steady research and thought he had put in (over about two months) had paid off. After that he 'saw' those horses regularly when doing this speech, but it wasn't as shocking as the first time – just a normal part of 'being' Richard II. (Incidentally, he had no idea of where this king fitted into English history when he started.)

When you are 'connecting' with your first line or two go on to the next, but use the first as a run up, and steadily on through the speech. (Please note that I still haven't suggested 'learning' the lines yet.)

I'm convinced that creating a character is very similar to the growing process from cradle to maturity.

Rehearsing Your Speeches

After you've done all this preparation you can start rehearsing your speeches, actually becoming the person saying those words in those particular circumstances. If you've prepared thoroughly, you'll be wonderfully surprised at how real, alive and exciting you can now make someone who was created four centuries ago.

Shakespeare's Advice

Hamlet says the following to a group of strolling players:

Speak the speech, I pray you, as I pronounced it to you – trippingly on the tongue; but if you mouth it, as many of your players do, I had as lief the town-crier had spoke my lines. Nor do not saw the air too much with your hand, thus, but use all gently; for in the very torrent, tempest, and as I may say the whirlwind of your passion, you must acquire and beget a temperance that may give it smoothness. O, it offends me to the soul to hear a robustious, periwig-pated fellow tear a passion to tatters, to very rags, to split the ears of the groundlings, who for the most part are capable of nothing but inexplicable dumb shows and noise ...

... Be not too tame, neither; but let your own discretion be your tutor. Suit the action to the word, the word to the action, with this special observance: that you o'erstep not the modesty of nature. For anything so overdone is from the purpose of playing, whose end, both at the first and now, was and is to hold as 'twere the mirror up to nature ... Now this overdone, or come tardy off, though it make the unskilful laugh, cannot but make the judicious grieve ...

(*Hamlet*, Act 2, Scene 3)

This is some of the most succinct acting advice ever given – three hundred years before Stanislavski (and others) were completely rethinking how we do acting.

The Speeches

All's Well That Ends Well

Countess of Rossillion

The Countess of Rossillion is the mother of Bertram and Helena is her ward. At this point the Countess knows of Helena's secret love for Bertram. Remembering her own youth, the Countess has great empathy with what Helena is going through and is very sympathetic to the idea of marriage. The women have been talking of their relationship; mildly quibbling over the words 'mother' and 'daughter'. Helena's (supposedly secret) concern is that Bertram cannot be seen as her 'brother', because if he were she could not marry him. At this point Helena has come closest to admitting her love.

The Countess could be as young as mid-thirties, but is generally played older.

---

2 *shield* forbid

3 *So strive upon your pulse* Make you nervous (when 'mother' and 'daughter' are mentioned)

4 *fondness* love (for Bertram)

6 *head* source
   gross obvious

7 *Invention* Your facility for making up excuses
   Against In the face of

13 *in their kind* in their own way

16 *clew* ball of thread (she is implying that Helena has 'wound' herself up into a state)

All's Well That Ends Well

Act 1, Scene 3
Countess –

1	Yes, Helen, you might be my daughter-in-law.
	God shield you mean it not! 'Daughter' and 'mother'
	So strive upon your pulse. What, pale again?
	My fear hath catched your fondness. Now I see
5	The mystery of your loneliness, and find
	Your salt tears' head. Now to all sense 'tis gross:
	You love my son. Invention is ashamed
	Against the proclamation of thy passion
	To say thou dost not. Therefore tell me true,
10	But tell me then 'tis so – for look, thy cheeks
	Confess it t' one to th' other, and thine eyes
	See it so grossly shown in thy behaviours
	That in their kind they speak it. Only sin
	And hellish obstinacy tie thy tongue,
15	That truth should be suspected. Speak, is 't so?
	If it be so, you have wound a goodly clew;
	If it be not, forswear 't. Howe'er, I charge thee,
	As heaven shall work in me for thine avail,
19	To tell me truly.

All's Well That Ends Well

Diana

Diana is a 'chaste' young woman living with her widowed mother in Florence. Bertram, a young French nobleman, has been making advances to her which she has previously resisted. He had earlier reluctantly promised to marry Helena (who has been brought up by his mother) on the orders of the King of France; however, he rushes straight off to the wars in Italy before the marriage is consummated. He writes to Helena saying that he will not acknowledge her as his wife until she wears his ring and bears his child. She follows him to Florence where she meets Diana and her mother, and stays with them. Helena tells the widow that she is Bertram's wife and the widow agrees to use her daughter as a decoy to get Helena into bed with him. In this scene Diana has agreed to sleep with Bertram (knowing Helena will in fact occupy her bed) if he will give her his ring, which he has just done.

---

2   *order take* make sure
3   *bond* (This is 'band' in some editions.)
9   *Another ring* (She is betokening the exchange of rings on engagement and marriage.)
12 *there my hope be done* this deed finishes my hopes (of becoming a wife)
12–13 (Bertram's line cut here; also his exit is marked here in many editions, rather than line 14)
17 *had* would have
19 *braid* twisted (as in braided hair)
20 *Marry that will* Let those marry who want to
21 *in this disguise* (i.e. by pretending to agree to sleep with Bertram)
22 *cozen* deceive

Act 4, Scene 2
Diana –

1 When midnight comes, knock at my chamber window,
   I'll order take my mother shall not hear.
   Now will I charge you in the bond of truth,
   When you have conquered my yet maiden bed,
5 Remain there but an hour, nor speak to me.
   My reasons are most strong, and you shall know them
   When back again this ring shall be delivered.
   And on your finger in the night I'll put
   Another ring that, what in time proceeds,
10 May token to the future our past deeds.
   Adieu till then; then, fail not. You have won
   A wife of me, though there my hope be done.
   For which live long to thank both heaven and me.
   You may so in the end.   *Exit Bertram*
15 My mother told me just how he would woo,
   As if she sat in 's heart. She says all men
   Have the like oaths. He had sworn to marry me
   When his wife's dead; therefore I'll lie with him
   When I am buried. Since Frenchmen are so braid,
20 Marry that will, I live and die a maid.
   Only, in this disguise, I think 't no sin
22 To cozen him that would unjustly win.   *Exit*

Antony And Cleopatra

Cleopatra, Queen of Egypt

Cleopatra, Queen of Egypt (68–30 B.C.) met Antony when she was 29. She had previously been the mistress of Julius Caesar and of Gnaeus Pompey – the younger son of Pompey the Great (Caesar's arch rival). She may be younger than is often perceived, but she is old in experience. Antony has been called back to Rome on urgent business. He has just appeared and has simply said, 'I am sorry to give breathing to my purpose –' when she's off with this pre-emptive strike, to try and stop him leaving Alexandria.

In the play Antony tries to interrupt her, I have simply cut his lines and slightly rearranged the verse.

———————————

3   *married woman* (i.e. Fulvia, Antony's wife)

8   *planted* placed ready

10 *Though you... gods* (When Jupiter, King of the gods, swore an oath, the whole of Olympus was supposed to shudder to its foundations.)

11 *Riotous madness* (i.e. 'for me')

12 *mouth-made* (i.e. just that and not from the heart)

13 *break themselves in swearing* are broken at the moment of 'swearing'

14 *colour* excuse

15 *sued staying* begged to stay

16 *Then was the time for words* Then your words really meant something

17–19 *Eternity... heaven.* (She is throwing Antony's past, honeyed words back in his face.)

17, 18 *our* (may be the royal plural but could also refer to the 'mutual pair')

18 *brows' bent* (the curve of the eyebrows – with a sexual implication. In some editions it's 'brow's', i.e. a singular possessive.)

    parts so poor qualities, however poor

19 *a race of heaven* of heavenly origins

22 *I would I had thy inches.* I wish I was as big (and strong) as you.

23 *a heart* courage

    Egypt (Cleopatra herself, as well as her country)

Act 1, Scene 3
Cleopatra –

1   Pray you, stand farther from me.
       I know by that same eye there's some good news.
       What says the married woman – you may go?
       Would she had never given you leave to come.
5   Let her not say 'tis I that keep you here.
       I have no power upon you; hers you are.
       Never was there queen so mightily betrayed!
       Yet at the first I saw the treasons planted.
       Why should I think you can be mine and true –
10   Though you in swearing shake the thronèd gods –
       Who have been false to Fulvia? Riotous madness,
       To be entangled with those mouth-made vows
       Which break themselves in swearing.
       Nay, pray you, seek no colour for your going,
15   But bid farewell and go. When you sued staying,
       Then was the time for words; no going then.
       Eternity was in our lips and eyes,
       Bliss in our brows' bent; none our parts so poor
       But was a race of heaven. They are so still,
20   Or thou, the greatest soldier of the world,
       Art turned the greatest liar.
       I would I had thy inches. Thou shouldst know
23   There were a heart in Egypt.

Antony and Cleopatra

Cleopatra, Queen of Egypt

Cleopatra, Queen of Egypt (68–30 B.C.) met Antony when she was 29. She had previously been the mistress of Julius Caesar and of Gnaeus Pompey – the younger son of Pompey the Great (Caesar's arch rival). She may be younger than is often perceived, but she is old in experience. She is with her handmaidens, Charmian and Iras, and is bemoaning Antony's absence.

---

5 *Do bravely* Go splendidly
   wot'st thou do you know

6 *demi-Atlas* (She is comparing Antony to Atlas, who in Greek mythology supported the heavens. Antony was also one of the three men who then ruled the Roman empire.)

6–7 *the arm / And burgonet of men* (i.e. the supreme soldier; 'arm' is attack and 'burgonet' is defence. A 'burgonet' was an exceptionally effective helmet of Burgundian origin.)

11 *Phoebus' amorous pinches black* deeply tanned from the 'pinches' of her lover *Phoebus* (the sun). (There is a strong implication that those 'pinches' are sexual – and that she has much experience of these.)

12 *wrinkled deep in time* (Humorously meant – she's lived a lot of life in a comparatively short time. There is a question mark at the end of this sentence in some editions.)
   Broad-fronted ('Front' can mean 'forehead' or 'face'. Julius Caesar apparently had 'a rather broad face'. I take it to imply strong and brave as in 'broad-chested'. Caesar also conquered many lands or 'fronts'.)

13 *here above the ground* still alive

14 *morsel for a monarch* tasty mouthful (The implication is that she was very young and inexperienced compared to Caesar.)

16 *aspect* (accented on the second syllable) gaze
   die (be consumed with sexual desire, even orgasm)

Act 1, Scene 5
Cleopatra –

1	O, Charmian,
	Where think'st thou he is now? Stands he or sits he?
	Or does he walk? Or is he on his horse?
	O happy horse, to bear the weight of Antony!
5	Do bravely, horse, for wot'st thou whom thou mov'st?
	The demi-Atlas of this earth, the arm
	And burgonet of men. He's speaking now,
	Or murmuring 'Where's my serpent of old Nile?'
	For so he calls me. Now I feed myself
10	With most delicious poison. Think on me,
	That am with Phoebus' amorous pinches black,
	And wrinkled deep in time. Broad-fronted Caesar,
	When thou wast here above the ground, I was
	A morsel for a monarch; and great Pompey
15	Would stand and make his eyes grow in my brow;
	There would he anchor his aspect, and die
17	With looking on his life.

The Comedy of Errors

The Courtesan

The Courtesan has been visited (off-stage) by Antipholus of *Ephesus* after he is mistakenly rejected by his wife, Adriana. The Courtesan entertains him to dinner and here arrives to claim a chain Antipholus promised her in exchange for her ring. However, she has mistakenly approached the wrong Antipholus (of *Syracuse*, the identical twin brother of Antipholus of *Ephesus*), who, not knowing what she is talking about, rejects her as a sorceress or agent of the devil. He is beginning to reach the end of his tether in this play of mistaken identity and his apparently 'mad' behaviour is born out of extreme frustration.

A 'Courtesan' is usually a high-class prostitute and can be any age you like – within reason.

In the play Antipholus (of *Syracuse*) and his servant have short sections of dialogue in between her lines (up to line 10). However, I think this works as a speech if you think of them as being struck dumb and appearing 'mad'. On the other hand you could just do the section from line 11, when she is left alone.

---

the *Porcupine*: there was both an inn and a brothel of this name in Shakespeare's London.
5   *mend* supplement, complete
7   *diamond* (i.e. it's a diamond 'ring')
13 *ducats* (Gold (or silver) coins, today worth about 50p, i.e. her 'forty ducats' is probably equivalent to at least several hundred pounds in modern terms; the silver ones were about a third of this value)
17 *rage* madness
20 *Belike* Probably
22 *My way* The best thing for me to do
    hie home go immediately
24 *perforce* forcibly

Act 4, Scene 3
Courtesan –

Enter a Courtesan from the Porcupine
1   Well met, well met, Master Antipholus.
     I see, sir, you have found the goldsmith now.
     Is that the chain you promised me today?
     Your man and you are marvellous merry, sir.
5   Will you go with me? We'll mend our dinner here.
     Give me the ring of mine you had at dinner,
     Or, for my diamond, the chain you promised,
     And I'll be gone, sir, and not trouble you.
     I pray you, sir, my ring, or else the chain.
10   I hope you do not mean to cheat me so?
     Exeunt Antipholus of Syracuse and his Servant
     Now, out of doubt, Antipholus is mad;
     Else would he never so demean himself.
     A ring he hath of mine worth forty ducats,
     And for the same he promised me a chain.
15   Both one and other he denies me now.
     The reason that I gather he is mad,
     Besides this present instance of his rage,
     Is a mad tale he told today at dinner
     Of his own doors being shut against his entrance.
20   Belike his wife, acquainted with his fits,
     On purpose shut the doors against his way.
     My way is now to hie home to his house,
     And tell his wife that, being lunatic,
     He rushed into my house, and took perforce
25   My ring away. This course I fittest choose,
     For forty ducats is too much to lose.   *Exit*

29

The Comedy of Errors

Aemilia, the Abbess

Aemilia (Emilia) is Abbess of Ephesus and doesn't appear until the final scene, largely ignorant of the chaos of mistaken identities that is the theme of the play. She is talking to Adriana, who thinks that her husband, who has been behaving very strangely recently, is inside the priory. Aemilia questions her about his strange behaviour and comes to this conclusion in this speech. (In fact, though neither Aemilia or Adriana realise it here, the man inside the priory is Adriana's husband's long-lost twin brother and it turns out that he is also Aemilia's long-lost son.)

Although she is generally played middle-aged or older Aemilia could be as young as early thirties.

----

2   *venom* venomous
4   *railing* abusive behaviour
5   *comes it that his head is light* it appears that he's mad
10 *sports* recreations
15 *distemperatures* illnesses
17 *would mad or man or beast* would madden either man or beast

Act 5, Scene 1
Abbess –

1   And thereof came it that the man was mad.
    The venom clamours of a jealous woman
    Poisons more deadly than a mad dog's tooth.
    It seems his sleeps were hindered by thy railing,
5   And thereof comes it that his head is light.
    Thou say'st his meat was sauced with thy upbraidings.
    Unquiet meals make ill digestions.
    Thereof the raging fire of fever bred,
    And what's a fever but a fit of madness?
10   Thou say'st his sports were hindered by thy brawls.
    Sweet recreation barred, what doth ensue
    But moody and dull melancholy,
    Kinsman to grim and comfortless despair,
    And at her heels a huge infectious troop
15   Of pale distemperatures and foes to life?
    In food, in sport, and life-preserving rest
    To be disturbed would mad or man or beast.
    The consequence is, then, thy jealous fits
19   Hath scared thy husband from the use of wits.

Coriolanus

Volumnia

Volumnia is an aristocratic Roman matron and the mother of Caius Martius (a Roman general), who is given the name 'Coriolanus' later in the play, after his victory over the Volscians. She is predominant over her son ('There's no man in the world / More bound to 's mother') and manages to persuade (even bully) him to do things against his own will as the play progresses. Her upbringing of him has made him the successful (and arrogant) warrior that he is. In this scene his wife, Virgilia, is fearful for her husband's safety, but Volumnia will have none of it, as in this speech.

Stage directions, which are probably not Shakespeare's, indicate that Virgilia and Volumnia are at home sewing.

Volumnia is probably in her mid-forties, but is generally played older.

This is two speeches put together, with a couple of sentences removed.

———————

1–2 *in a more comfortable sort* more cheerfully
6 *comeliness* good looks
7–8 *when for a day of kings' entreaties* even for the most important reasons
8 *should* would
   sell lose
9–10 *such a person* such a handsome man
10 *it* this handsome man
10–11 *hang by th' wall* be mere decoration
11 *if renown made it not stir* if the possibility of fame did not motivate it
12 *like* likely
13–14 *brows bound with oak* crowned with a garland of oak leaves (the Roman reward for saving the life of a comrade)
19 *voluptuously surfeit* spend his time in excessive self-indulgence
20 *out of action* avoiding battle

Act 1, Scene 3
Volumnia –

1   I pray you, daughter, sing, or express yourself in a more
       comfortable sort. If my son were my husband, I should
       freelier rejoice in that absence wherein he won honour,
       than in the embracements of his bed where he would show
5   most love. When yet he was but tender-bodied, and the
       only son of my womb; when youth with comeliness
       plucked all gaze his way; when for a day of kings'
       entreaties, a mother should not sell him an hour from her
       beholding; I, considering how honour would become such
10   a person – that it was no better than, picture-like to hang by
       th' wall, if renown made it not stir – was pleased to let him
       seek danger where he was like to find fame. To a cruel war
       I sent him, from whence he returned his brows bound with
       oak. I tell thee, daughter, I sprang not more in joy at first
15   hearing he was a man-child, than now in first seeing he
       had proved himself a man. Hear me profess sincerely: had
       I a dozen sons, each in my love alike, and none less dear
       than thine and my good Martius', I had rather had eleven
       die nobly for their country than one voluptuously surfeit
20   out of action.

Coriolanus

Valeria

Valeria is a friend of Coriolanus' wife, Virgilia. Before Valeria arrives, Volumnia (Coriolanus' mother) has upset her daughter-in-law by her telling how honourable it is that Coriolanus has gone to war; Virgilia can only think of the threat to his safety and she doesn't really want to talk to anyone. The naturally jolly Valeria does her best to lighten the atmosphere. She has three other scenes (accompanying Virgilia) in which she hardly says another word. In spite of her chattiness in this scene she is described later as a particularly noble Roman woman. She can be anywhere in her twenties or thirties.

Stage directions, which are probably not Shakespeare's, indicate that Virgilia and Volumnia are at home sewing.

Although she addresses both Virgilia and Volumnia at the beginning, the bulk of Valeria's following remarks are for Virgilia.

The Roman names in this speech are pronounced exactly as written, sounding every letter in the word.

---

2   *manifest housekeepers* obviously staying at home
3   *fine spot* finely worked embroidery (probably a pattern of small flowers, fruits, and the like)
6   *confirmed countenance* determined look
7   *gilded* shining with all kinds of colours (like a petrol film in bright light)
8   *over and over* head over heels
10 *set* clenched tightly
11 *mammocked* tore to shreds
     la (an exclamation calling attention to an emphatic statement; also on line 19)
15 *Penelope* (The wife of Ulysses, King of Ithaca. During his long absence after the siege of Troy, and presuming him dead, she was pressed to marry one of her many suitors. She put them off by pretending that she could not marry until she had finished a shroud she was weaving. At night she undid the work she had done in the day, so that it was never finished.)
16 *moths* (both the insects and in the sense of 'parasites' – referring to the suitors of Penelope who lived in the house of Ulysses and consumed his goods)
17 *cambric* (A fine linen, named after Cambray in Flanders, where it was first made.)
     sensible as sensitive
18 *leave pricking it for pity* take pity on the cloth and leave it
22 *Volsces* (pronounced *Vol-skeyz*)
23 & 24 *Cominius & Titus Lartius* (Coriolanus' fellow generals)
24 *power* fighting force
25–6 *They nothing doubt prevailing, and to make it brief wars.* They are confident of victory and the campaign will be brief.

Act 1, Scene 3
Valeria –

1   My ladies both, good day to you. How do you both? You
       are manifest housekeepers. What are you sewing here? A
       fine spot, in good faith. How does your little son? O' my
       word, the father's son! I'll swear 'tis a very pretty boy. O'
5   my troth, I looked upon him o' Wednesday half an hour
       together. He's such a confirmed countenance! I saw him
       run after a gilded butterfly, and when he caught it he let it
       go again, and after it again, and over and over he comes,
       and up again, catched it again. Or whether his fall enraged
10   him, or how 'twas, he did so set his teeth and tear it! O, I
       warrant, how he mammocked it! Indeed, la, 'tis a noble
       child. Come, lay aside your stitchery. I must have you play
       the idle housewife with me this afternoon. Fie, you confine
       yourself most unreasonably. You would be another
15   Penelope. Yet they say all the yarn she spun in Ulysses'
       absence did but fill Ithaca full of moths. Come, I would
       your cambric were sensible as your finger, that you might
       leave pricking it for pity. Come, you shall go with us. In
       truth, la, go with me, and I'll tell you excellent news of
20   your husband. Verily, I do not jest with you: there came
       news from him last night. In earnest, it's true. I heard a
       senator speak it. Thus it is: the Volsces have an army forth,
       against whom Cominius the general is gone with one part
       of our Roman power. Your lord and Titus Lartius are set
25   down before their city Corioles. They nothing doubt
       prevailing, and to make it brief wars. This is true, on mine
       honour; and so, I pray, go with us. Prithee, Virgilia, turn
28   thy solemness out o' door and go along with us.

Cymbeline

The Queen of Britain

The Queen of Britain is the wife of King Cymbeline and stepmother of his daughter Imogen, and mother (by a former marriage) of the oafish Cloten. She wants to see him married to Imogen so as to secure the throne for him. However, Imogen has secretly married Posthumus and when this is discovered he is banished. His faithful servant, Pisanio, stays behind to serve her. The Queen has just received (what she believes) is a potent poison from a doctor (Cornelius) and he has asked her why she wants these 'most poisonous compounds'.

Although King Cymbeline really existed (generally called Cunobelius) around two thousand years ago, we know nothing about his real queen. She could be any age from early thirties to early fifties.

It isn't clear what her immediate motivation for wanting the poison is, so you have to make up your own mind.

I have cut the doctor's lines (between 'effects.' and 'Content' in line 14) and an 'O' (in the same line) to keep the metre.

---

3   *learned* taught
6   *confections* concoctions of drugs
9   *conclusions* experiments
13 *Allayments* Antidotes
    act action
    gather draw conclusions
14 *Content thee* Set your mind at rest
16 *He's factor for* (The word 'factor' was added by an editor – I like it, but it doesn't appear in some editions.)

Act 1, Scene 6 (Scene 5 in some editions)
Queen –

1 I wonder, doctor,
  Thou ask'st me such a question. Have I not been
  Thy pupil long? Hast thou not learned me how
  To make perfumes, distil, preserve – yea, so
5 That our great King himself doth woo me oft
  For my confections? Having thus far proceeded,
  Unless thou think'st me devilish, is 't not meet
  That I did amplify my judgement in
  Other conclusions? I will try the forces
10 Of these thy compounds on such creatures as
  We count not worth the hanging, but none human,
  To try the vigour of them, and apply
  Allayments to their act, and by them gather
  Their several virtues and effects. Content thee.
  Enter Pisanio
15 [*Aside*] Here comes a flattering rascal; upon him
  Will I first work. He's factor for his master,
  And enemy to my son. [*Aloud*] How now, Pisanio? –
  Doctor, your service for this time is ended.
19 Take your own way.

Henry IV, part 2

Doll Tearsheet

Doll Tearsheet is a prostitute, mistress of Sir John Falstaff and a regular at the Boar's Head Tavern with him, Pistol and Mistress Quickly (the Hostess). She can be very sentimental (especially with Falstaff) and extremely pugnacious (as here) – she is also described as 'a proper gentlewoman'. Pistol has just made a sexual advance.

She could be any age from late teens to late thirties.

I have cut several lines of Pistol, Mistress Quickly and Falstaff to construct this speech.

———————————

2   *lack-linen* scruffy
    mate fellow
3   *master* (i.e. Falstaff)
4   *bung* pickpocket
5   *chaps* cheeks
5–6 *an you play the saucy cuttle* if you play any of your tricks
7   *bottle-ale* (implying 'cheap', from 'small-beer' or 'frothy')
    basket-hilt (Literally, a sword hilt with curved steel strips, in a basket shape, to protect the hand; but she's using it contemptuously, because such extra protection was for cowards or simply for show.)
    stale old-fashioned
    juggler impostor
8   *Since when* Since when have you become a soldier?
9   *points* laces (used for securing armour). (She's implying that he is dressed more impressively than he behaves.)
    Much! (An expression of scornful incredulity like, 'What?!')
11 *An* If
12 *truncheon you out* beat you out of the ranks with truncheons (which captains carried as signs of authority).
    for taking their names upon you for assuming the title of 'captain'
14 *tearing a poor whore's ruff* (Pistol has just threatened to do this)
15–16 *stewed prunes* (Prunes were thought to be a cure for venereal disease, and 'stews' were brothels.)
16 *dried cakes* (cakes need to be kept moist)
17 *'occupy'* 'fornicate'
18 *ill-sorted* in bad company

38

Act 2, Scene 4
Doll –

1   I scorn you, scurvy companion. What, you poor, base, rascally, cheating, lack-linen mate! Away, you mouldy rogue, away! I am meat for your master. Away, you cutpurse rascal, you filthy bung, away! By this wine, I'll

5   thrust my knife in your mouldy chaps an you play the saucy cuttle with me! [*She brandishes a knife*] Away, you bottle-ale rascal, you basket-hilt stale juggler, you! [*Pistol draws his sword*] Since when, I pray you, sir? God's light, with two points on your shoulder! Much! Captain? Thou

10   abominable damned cheater, art thou not ashamed to be called 'captain'? An captains were of my mind, they would truncheon you out, for taking their names upon you before you have earned them. You a captain? You slave! For what? For tearing a poor whore's ruff in a bawdy-house! He a

15   captain? Hang him, rogue, he lives upon mouldy stewed prunes and dried cakes. A captain? God's light, these villains will make the word as odious as the word 'occupy', which was an excellent good word before it was ill-sorted.

19   Therefore captains had need look to 't.

Henry VI, part 1

The Countess of Auvergne

The Countess of Auvergne only appears in this one scene, which has no basis in historical record – so she can be almost any age you would like her to be. All we know from the play before this is that she has invited the English hero Talbot to her castle, pretending an innocent desire to meet so brave a soldier. In fact, she is trying to entrap him through her trickery – it doesn't work because he has secretly brought soldiers with him. After this speech she acknowledges his cleverness and even invites him to a banquet – and we never see her again.

We are not specifically told of the details of the Countess' plot – to play her you have to work out what it could be for yourself.

I have put three short speeches together to construct this one.

----

1   *gave in charge* ordered
5   *Tomyris* (A Scythian queen who defeated Cyrus' army of 200,000 Persians. She threw his head into a wine-skin full of human blood, in revenge for his slaying of her son and to symbolise his blood-thirstiness.)
6   *dreadful* frightening
8   *Fain* Hopefully
9   *give their censure of* contradict
11 *abroad* everywhere
12 *still* silence
13 *fabulous* mythical
15 *for* because of
     aspect facial appearance
17 *seely* feeble (Some editions have 'silly', but I prefer the sound of 'seely'.)
18 *writhled* wrinkled

Act 2, Scene 3
Countess –

     Auvergne. The castle. Enter the Countess and her Porter.
1   Porter, remember what I gave in charge,
     And when you have done so, bring the keys to me.
                          Porter exits
     The plot is laid. If all things fall out right,
     I shall as famous be by this exploit
5   As Scythian Tomyris by Cyrus' death.
     Great is the rumour of this dreadful knight,
     And his achievements of no less account.
     Fain would mine eyes be witness with mine ears,
     To give their censure of these rare reports.
     Enter Lord Talbot
10   Is this the man? Is this the scourge of France?
     Is this the Talbot, so much feared abroad
     That with his name the mothers still their babes?
     I see report is fabulous and false.
     I thought I should have seen some Hercules,
15   A second Hector, for his grim aspect
     And large proportion of his strong-knit limbs.
     Alas, this is a child, a seely dwarf.
     It cannot be this weak and writhled shrimp
19   Should strike such terror to his enemies.

Henry VI, part 2

Duchess of Gloucester, Eleanor Cobham

The Duchess of Gloucester, Eleanor Cobham, was the wife of Duke Humphrey of Gloucester (1390–1447). Humphrey was the youngest son of King Henry IV and brother of King Henry V, and had been 'Protector of England', whilst his nephew Henry VI was a child. Humphrey was still at this time (historically 1441) next in line to the throne as all his brothers were dead and Henry VI though now in his twenties had no children. Eleanor was first Humphrey's mistress and then his second wife and we know very little else about the real lady beyond the fact that she was arrested and tried on the (possibly trumped up) charges of 'necromancy, witchcraft, heresy, and treason'. Shakespeare's Eleanor could be any age above about 25. She is an ambitious woman and has every reason to encourage her husband to attempt to seize the throne from the childless and weak Henry VI.

---

2   *Ceres* (the Roman goddess of the harvest)
    plenteous load rich harvest
5   *sullen* gloomy
8   *Enchased* Adorned with
9   *grovel on thy face* (This is part of the witchcraft ceremony.)
12 *is 't* (i.e. 'is your arm')
15 *abase* lower
16 *vouchsafe* grant condescendingly

Act 1, Scene 2
Duchess of Gloucester –

The Duke of Gloucester's house.
Enter Duke Humphrey and his wife Eleanor.

1   Why droops my lord, like over-ripened corn
    Hanging the head at Ceres' plenteous load?
    Why doth the great Duke Humphrey knit his brows,
    As frowning at the favours of the world?
5   Why are thine eyes fixed to the sullen earth,
    Gazing on that which seems to dim thy sight?
    What seest thou there? King Henry's diadem,
    Enchased with all the honours of the world?
    If so, gaze on, and grovel on thy face
10   Until thy head be circled with the same.
    Put forth thy hand, reach at the glorious gold.
    What, is 't too short? I'll lengthen it with mine;
    And having both together heaved it up,
    We'll both together lift our heads to heaven,
15   And never more abase our sight so low
16   As to vouchsafe one glance unto the ground.

Henry VI, part 2

Duchess of Gloucester, Eleanor Cobham

The Duchess of Gloucester, Eleanor Cobham, was the wife of Duke Humphrey of Gloucester (1390–1447). Humphrey was the youngest son of King Henry IV and brother of King Henry V, and had been 'Protector of England', whilst his nephew Henry VI was a child. Humphrey was still at this time (historically 1441) next in line to the throne as all his brothers were dead and Henry VI though now in his twenties had no children. Eleanor was first Humphrey's mistress and then his second wife and we know very little else about the real lady beyond the fact that she was arrested and tried on the (possibly trumped up) charges of 'necromancy, witchcraft, heresy, and treason'. Shakespeare's Eleanor could be any age above about 25. She is an ambitious woman and has every reason to encourage her husband to attempt to seize the throne from the childless and weak Henry VI.

At this point she is being paraded ignominiously through the streets as part of her punishment for invoking evil spirits. Humphrey is waiting for her and says, 'Be patient, gentle Nell; forget this grief'. This is her response.

———————————

5   *Mailed up* Enveloped
    papers on my back (These are the *'verses pinned on her back'* which describe the nature of her crimes.)
7   *deep-fet* fetched up from deep inside myself
8   *ruthless flint* (flint is a very hard, sharp stone, then used in primitive road-making)
9   *start* flinch (with the pain)
10 *be advisèd* be careful
12 *Trowest thou* Do you believe
19 *As* That
20 *pointing-stock* (object to be pointed at with scorn; like 'laughing-stock')
25 *Suffolk* (William de la Pole, Duke of Suffolk – a very ambitious noble, very much in the ascendant at this time. Shakespeare makes him Queen Margaret's lover.)
26 *her* (Queen Margaret)
27 *York* (Richard Plantagenet, Duke of York – distant cousin of the King)
    Beaufort (Bishop of Winchester and great uncle to the King)
28 *limed* smeared with bird-lime (twigs were 'limed' to catch young birds)
29 *fly thou how thou canst* no matter how much you try to fly away
    tangle ensnare
30 (She is being sarcastic about her husband's unsuspecting nature.)
31 *seek prevention of* take action to pre-empt (the schemes)

Act 2, Scene 4
Duchess of Gloucester –

Enter the Duchess, Dame Eleanor Cobham, barefoot, with a
white sheet about her, written verses pinned on her back, and
carrying a wax candle in her hand; she is accompanied by the
Sheriff of London and officers

1   Ah, Gloucester, teach me to forget myself;
    For whilst I think I am thy married wife,
    And thou a prince, Protector of this land,
    Methinks I should not thus be led along,
5   Mailed up in shame, with papers on my back,
    And followed with a rabble that rejoice
    To see my tears and hear my deep-fet groans.
    The ruthless flint doth cut my tender feet,
    And when I start, the envious people laugh,
10 And bid me be advisèd how I tread.
    Ah, Humphrey, can I bear this shameful yoke?
    Trowest thou that e'er I'll look upon the world,
    Or count them happy that enjoy the sun?
    No, dark shall be my light, and night my day;
15 To think upon my pomp shall be my hell.
    Sometime I'll say I am Duke Humphrey's wife,
    And he a prince and ruler of the land;
    Yet so he ruled, and such a prince he was,
    As he stood by whilst I, his forlorn Duchess,
20 Was made a wonder and a pointing-stock
    To every idle rascal follower.
    But be thou mild and blush not at my shame,
    Nor stir at nothing till the axe of death
    Hang over thee, as sure it shortly will;
25 For Suffolk, he that can do all in all
    With her that hateth thee and hates us all,
    And York, and impious Beaufort, that false priest,
    Have all limed bushes to betray thy wings,
    And fly thou how thou canst, they'll tangle thee.
30 But fear not thou until thy foot be snared,
    Nor never seek prevention of thy foes.

Henry VI, part 3

Lady Gray (Elizabeth Woodville)

Lady Gray (Elizabeth Woodville, 1437(?)–1492) was the first commoner to become Queen of England. She married Edward IV (successor to Henry VI) after the death of her first husband at the battle of St. Albans. She is a pawn in the troubled politics of the time. She has just heard that the King, her husband, has been captured and she is talking to her brother.

Historically the events referred to took place when she was in her early thirties.

Lady Gray also appears in Richard III. Some editions refer to her as Queen Elizabeth, which was technically correct at this time. Gray is sometimes spelt Grey.

This speech is constructed from several shorter ones and I have also made some minor word changes.

———————————

2   *late* recent
5   *surprised* taken prisoner
    at unawares caught unawares
6   *have to* am given to
7   *new committed to* recently placed in the custody of
8   *Warwick* (known as the 'King-maker'. A very powerful noble and brilliant soldier who had strong influence on the running of the country. Initially he was an ally of Edward's, but fell out with him over his marriage to Elizabeth. Warwick had planned a political marriage for him to strengthen his position. He subsequently ruled England for nine months.)
12 *bridle* keep control of
14 *draw in* hold back (from the brink)
15 *blood-sucking sighs* (It was believed that every sigh drew a drop of blood from the heart.)
16 *blast* destroy
19 *Henry* (King Henry VI (whom Edward had deposed, with the help of Warwick, ten years earlier))
20 *must down* will lose their power, wealth and influence (and possibly their lives)
23 *sanctuary* (a religious house where residence guaranteed immunity from arrest)
24 *right* just claim to the crown

Act 4, Scene 4 (Scene 5 in some editions)
Lady Gray –

    Enter Earl Rivers and his sister, Lady Gray, Edward's queen.
1   Why, brother Rivers, you are yet to learn
    What late misfortune is befall'n King Edward.
    He's almost slain – for he is taken prisoner,
    Either betrayed by falsehood of his guard
5   Or by his foe surprised at unawares;
    And, as I further have to understand,
    Is new committed to the Bishop of York,
    Fell Warwick's brother, and by that our foe.
    Now then fair hope must hinder life's decay;
10   And I the rather wean me from despair
    For love of Edward's offspring in my womb.
    This is it that makes me bridle passion
    And bear with mildness my misfortune's cross.
    Ah me, for this I draw in many a tear
15   And stop the rising of blood-sucking sighs,
    Lest with my sighs or tears I blast or drown
    King Edward's fruit, true heir to th' English crown.
    I am informèd Warwick comes towards London
    To set the crown once more on Henry's head.
20   Guess thou the rest – King Edward's friends must down.
    But to prevent the tyrant's violence –
    For trust not him that hath once broken faith –
    I'll hence forthwith unto the sanctuary,
    To save at least the heir of Edward's right.
25   There shall I rest secure from force and fraud.
    Come, therefore, let us fly while we may fly.
27   If Warwick take us, we are sure to die.   *Exeunt*

Henry VIII

Anne Boleyn

Anne Boleyn (Bullen) (c. 1507–1536) was Henry VIII's second wife and mother of Elizabeth I. At this point (when she is about 20) there is rumour of Henry divorcing his first wife, Katherine of Aragon, in favour of Anne. (She was a maid of honour to Katherine.) In reality she seems to have been extremely devious, compared to the high-principled lady in Shakespeare's play. Perhaps he couldn't tell the truth about the mother of the then still-popular Queen Elizabeth who had only died ten years previously. She seems here to be very innocent – however, given that this is the only scene in which she has any sustained dialogue (she doesn't even speak at her coronation and is not present at the christening of Elizabeth) I think it is possible to play this speech as someone putting up a 'public front'. Although, she is apparently alone with the Old Lady, the 'devious' lady of reality would know that there were spies everywhere. On the other hand I have seen her successfully performed completely straightforwardly.

I have constructed this speech from several shorter ones.

---

1 *pang that pinches* nags at my conscience
4 *Pronounce* Make known publicly
6 *courses of the sun enthronèd* years as queen (about 18 at this point)
9 *this process* all this time (virtuously spent)
10 *give her the avaunt* reject her
   pity cause for pity.
12 *temporal* merely earthly (i.e. not religious)
13 *quarrel* quarreller
14 *sufferance panging* suffering as painful
18 *range with humble livers* live amongst ordinary people ('livers' = people who live)
19 *perked up in a glist'ring grief* made to look good on the outside whilst grieving inside
20 *a golden sorrow* a crown (with all the problems that would bring)
21 *Maidenhead* Virginity

Henry VIII

Act 2, Scene 3
Anne –

Enter Anne Boleyn and an Old Lady
1 Not for that neither. Here's the pang that pinches:
His highness having lived so long with her, and she
So good a lady that no tongue could ever
Pronounce dishonour of her – by my life,
5 She never knew harm-doing. O now, after
So many courses of the sun enthronèd,
Still growing in a majesty and pomp, the which
To leave a thousand-fold more bitter than
'Tis sweet at first t' acquire. After this process,
10 To give her the avaunt, it is a pity
Would move a monster. O, God's will! Much better
She ne'er had known pomp; though 't be temporal,
Yet if that quarrel, fortune, do divorce
It from the bearer, 'tis a sufferance panging
15 As soul and body's severing. So much the more
Must pity drop upon her. Verily,
I swear, 'tis better to be lowly born
And range with humble livers in content,
Than to be perked up in a glist'ring grief
20 And wear a golden sorrow. By my troth and
Maidenhead, I would not be a queen.

Henry VIII

Katherine of Aragon

Katherine of Aragon, Queen of England (1485–1536), was the first wife of Henry VIII. She only had one surviving child (Mary) and after twenty years of marriage, Henry, desperate for a male heir and with an eye for Anne Boleyn, institutes divorce proceedings based on a disputed reading of catholic church law. She refuses to accept the idea and here Cardinals Wolsey and Campeius are trying to get her to change her mind. They have just arrived and Wolsey has just suggested that they go into her 'private chamber'. She declares that she has nothing to hide.

Although she was Spanish by birth, she had lived in England for most of her adult life, so she could have a slight accent. She was forty-three at the time.

In the play Wolsey speaks his 'Latin' between lines 11 and 12 (which her waiting-women would not have understood); I have simply presumed that she knows he is prone to do this and pre-empts him. I have also slightly changed line 12.

Her wonderful courtroom speeches (Act 2, Scene 4) are very often used in audition.

---

3   *Deserves a corner* Needs to be kept secret
4   *free* innocent
6   *a number* most other people
8   *base opinion* cheap gossip
9   *so even* completely blameless
10   *that way I am wife in* how I behave as a wife
14   *such a truant* so lazy
16   *strange tongue* foreign language
     more strange, suspicious more strange (or foreign), even suspicious
20   *willing'st* most deliberate

Act 3, Scene 1
Queen Katherine –

1   Speak it here.
    There's nothing I have done yet, o' my conscience,
    Deserves a corner. Would all other women
    Could speak this with as free a soul as I do.
5   My lords, I care not – so much I am happy
    Above a number – if my actions
    Were tried by every tongue, every eye saw 'em,
    Envy and base opinion set against 'em,
    I know my life so even. If your business
10   Seek me out and that way I am wife in,
    Out with it boldly. Truth loves open dealing.
    And, good my lord, no Latin!
    I am not such a truant since my coming
15   As not to know the language I have lived in.
    A strange tongue makes my cause more strange, suspicious;
    Pray, speak in English. Here are some will thank you,
    If you speak truth, for their poor mistress' sake.
    Believe me, she has had much wrong. Lord Cardinal,
20   The willing'st sin I ever yet committed
    May be absolved in English.

Henry VIII

Katherine of Aragon

Katherine of Aragon, Queen of England (1485–1536), was the first wife of Henry VIII. She only had one surviving child (Mary) and after twenty years of marriage, Henry, desperate for a male heir and with an eye for Anne Boleyn, divorced her. She never accepted this (it was based on a disputed reading of catholic church law); nevertheless, Henry allowed her to live out her life in some comfort. This is from her last scene of the play and she is giving her instructions to Capuchius (an ambassador from Rome and her nephew), who has been sent (too late) by Henry to wish her better health.

Although she was Spanish by birth, she had lived in England for most of her adult life, so she could have a slight accent.

Her wonderful courtroom speeches (Act 2, Scene 4) are very often used in audition.

---

4   *model* image of
    daughter (Mary Tudor, who was later Queen from 1553 to 1558. She was twenty at this time.)
6   *virtuous breeding* a good upbringing
8   *deserve well* be treated as well as she is entitled to be
8–9 *and a little / To love her* and (at least) love her a little (for my sake)
13 *both my fortunes* my fortunes both good and bad (i.e. her good 'fortune' as Queen and her current bad)
14 *avow* strongly declare
15 *now I should not lie* (It was commonly believed that people spoke the truth just before dying.)
17 *decent carriage* proper conduct
18 *Let him be* Make sure he is (She doesn't want her disgrace to spoil their prospects.)
20 *the poorest* in the worst position (as they couldn't marry wealth)
21 *draw 'em from me* make them leave me
25 *able* sufficient

Act 4, Scene 2
Queen Katherine –

1   [*To Capuchius*] Sir, I most humbly pray you to deliver
     This to my lord the King. [*She gives the letter to Capuchius*]
     In which I have commended to his goodness
     The model of our chaste loves, his young daughter –
5   The dews of heaven fall thick in blessings on her –
     Beseeching him to give her virtuous breeding.
     She is young, and of a noble modest nature.
     I hope she will deserve well – and a little
     To love her for her mother's sake, that loved him,
10   Heaven knows how dearly. My next poor petition
     Is that his noble grace would have some pity
     Upon my wretched women, that so long
     Have followed both my fortunes faithfully;
     Of which there is not one, I dare avow –
15   And now I should not lie – but will deserve,
     For virtue and true beauty of the soul,
     For honesty and decent carriage,
     A right good husband. Let him be a noble,
     And sure those men are happy that shall have 'em.
20   The last is for my men – they are the poorest,
     But poverty could never draw 'em from me –
     That they may have their wages duly paid 'em,
     And something over to remember me by.
     If heaven had pleased to have given me longer life,
25   And able means, we had not parted thus.
     These are the whole contents; and, good my lord,
     By that you love the dearest in this world,
     As you wish Christian peace to souls departed,
     Stand these poor people's friend and urge the King
30   To do me this last rite.

Julius Caesar

Calphurnia

Calphurnia was the wife of Julius Caesar, whom she married in 59 B.C., fifteen years before his assassination. Although Caesar was blatantly unfaithful (with Cleopatra for one) and came close to divorcing her (in order to make another political marriage), Calphurnia was seen by contemporaries to have been a genuinely devoted wife. After the assassination, she helped Mark Antony's campaign against the conspirators by turning over to him Caesar's papers and a large amount of cash. Unfortunately we know very little else about her, and I suggest that she could be anywhere between early thirties and middle fifties (Caesar was 58 at the time). In the play she only appears in this scene and in Act 1, Scene 2 – where she has one brief line. Just before this entrance Caesar ('in his night-gown') has said 'Thrice hath Calphurnia in her sleep cried out, "Help, ho! They murder Caesar!"'. There is also 'Thunder and lightning' raging in the background.

I have cut Caesar's and a servant's lines to construct this speech.

You could simply go as far as line 16.

————————————

3   *stood on ceremonies* believed in omens
9   *fight* (This is 'fought' in some editions, but I prefer the present tense as she becomes more involved in what she's talking about.)
10 *right form of war* regular battle-order
12 *hurtled* clamoured
13 *do* (This is 'did' in some editions – see note on line 9.)
15 *beyond all use* beyond all normal experience
18 *consumed in confidence* being blinded by over-confidence

54

Act 2, Scene 2
Calphurnia –

Enter Calphurnia
1 What mean you, Caesar? Think you to walk forth?
You shall not stir out of your house today.
Caesar, I never stood on ceremonies,
Yet now they fright me. There is one within,
5 Besides the things that we have heard and seen,
Recounts most horrid sights seen by the watch.
A lioness hath whelpèd in the streets,
And graves have yawned and yielded up their dead.
Fierce fiery warriors fight upon the clouds,
10 In ranks and squadrons and right form of war,
Which drizzled blood upon the Capitol.
The noise of battle hurtled in the air.
Horses do neigh, and dying men did groan,
And ghosts did shriek and squeal about the streets.
15 O Caesar, these things are beyond all use,
And I did fear them.
Alas, my lord,
Your wisdom is consumed in confidence.
Do not go forth today. Call it my fear
20 That keeps you in the house, and not your own.
We'll send Mark Antony to the Senate House,
And he shall say you are not well today.
23 Let me upon my knee prevail in this.   *She kneels*

King Lear

Cordelia

Cordelia is King Lear's youngest and most virtuous daughter, whom he mistakenly rejects. In the first scene of the play, knowing she will marry, Cordelia refuses to assert that all of her love will forever go to her father (as he demands), unlike Regan and Goneril, her hypocritical sisters. Lear mistakes Cordelia's honesty for a lack of affection and disinherits her. She marries the King of France and is not seen again until Act 4, when she arrives with an army to help her father recover his throne. She finds the once proud man in a desperate physical and mental state.

There is more than one viable version of this play-text. The 'Folio' is the most authoritative one, but the 'Quarto' edition contains some extra lines (and detailed variations) that are now generally incorporated into the published versions of the play.

This is such a famous play that it is important that you are prepared to justify the performance decisions you make with this speech.

You could start this speech from 'O my dear father...'

----

3 *The untuned and jarring senses* (The slackened 'strings' of his mind are no longer 'in tune' but 'jar' against one another.)
    wind up 'tune' by tightening the strings ('wind' is as 'turn', not the weather)
    jarring (This is 'hurrying' in some editions.)

4 *child-changèd* (a) changed (to madness) by the cruelties of his children, (b) changed into second childishness

5 *[To Lear]* (Lear has either been there all the time (asleep) or carried in for this moment – for the purposes of an audition you can choose which suits you.)

9 *white flakes* snow-white hair

10 *challenge* demand

11 *warring* (The Folio edition has 'jarring' – again, choose which you would prefer.)

14 *cross lightning* forked lightning
    perdu (A 'sentinelle perdue' was an especially daring soldier who was placed (as a spy or a scout) so close to the enemy that it was generally a suicide mission.)

15 *thin helm* the thin hair (of an old man)

15–17 *Mine enemy's... fire.* I would have treated even such a dog better than Lear has been treated.

17 *fain* glad

19 *short and musty straw* (Long dry straw made the most comfortable bed; short is prickly and musty is damp.)

21 *all* at the same time

Act 4, Scene 7 (Scene 21 in the Quarto edition)
Cordelia –

> *A Tent in the French Camp.*
> *Cordelia with Kent, Doctor and Gentleman.*

1   O you kind gods,
       Cure this great breach in his abusèd nature;
       The untuned and jarring senses, O, wind up
       Of this child-changèd father!
5   [*To Lear*] O my dear father, restoration hang
       Thy medicine on my lips, and let this kiss
       Repair those violent harms that my two sisters
       Have in thy reverence made!
       Had you not been their father, these white flakes
10   Did challenge pity of them. Was this a face
       To be exposed against the warring winds,
       To stand against the deep dread-bolted thunder,
       In the most terrible and nimble stroke
       Of quick cross-lightning, to watch – poor *perdu* –
15   With this thin helm? Mine enemy's dog,
       Though he had bit me, should have stood that night
       Against my fire. And wast thou fain, poor father,
       To hovel thee with swine and rogues forlorn
       In short and musty straw? Alack, alack,
20   'Tis wonder that thy life and wits at once
21   Had not concluded all! [*To the Doctor*] He wakes. Speak to
           him.

Love's Labour's Lost

Mote

Mote (sometimes 'Moth') is a young page to Don Adriano de Armado, a pedantic and pompous Spaniard. Mote spends the play ridiculing his master, subtly to his face and blatantly behind his back. Armado is infatuated with Jacquenetta and Mote has just suggested that his master might win her with a 'French brawl' (which is a dance) – Armado takes this to mean a brawl (i.e. quarrel) in French; Mote puts him right with this speech.

Mote can be played by either a man or a woman.

---

1   *jig off a tune*   sing some jig-like (bright and lively) tune
2   *canary*   (lively Spanish dance)
3–6   *sigh... love*   (All these are demonstrations of love.)
4   *sometime*   at times
7   *penthouse-like*   like a projecting roof (i.e. making him look melancholy)
8   *thin-belly doublet*   doublet covering a thin belly (i.e. suggesting someone wasted through pining for love)
9   *after*   in the style of. (We don't know of any specific 'old painting' that Mote refers to.)
10–11   *snip and away*   a snatch and then on to another
11   *complements*   proper manners
      humours   moods
12   *betray*   attract
      nice   coy
      be betrayed   not be attracted (and 'feel let down')
13   *of note*   of distinction
13–14   *do you note me?*   (There are several variations on this line in different editions; this version seems the most appropriate to me.)
14   *affected*   inclined
      to these   (i.e. 'complements and humours')

Act 3, Scene 1
Mote –

1   No, my complete master; but to jig off a tune at the
tongue's end, canary to it with your feet, humour it with
turning up your eyelids, sigh a note and sing a note,
sometime through the throat as if you swallowed love
5   with singing love, sometime through the nose as if you
snuffed up love by smelling love; with your hat
penthouse-like o'er the shop of your eyes; with your arms
crossed on your thin-belly doublet like a rabbit on a spit;
or your hands in your pocket like a man after the old
10   painting; and keep not too long in one tune, but a snip
and away. These are complements, these are humours;
these betray nice wenches, that would be betrayed
without these; and make them men of note – do you note
14   me? – that most are affected to these.

Love's Labour's Lost

The Princess of France

The Princess of France (we're never given a first name) is a very sharp, witty and straightforward lady. Technically, she is on a diplomatic mission to the King of Navarre (now part in France and part in Spain) with her three attendant ladies. 'Diplomacy ' turns to fun and much of the play is spent in verbal flirtations and battles of wits between the women and the King and his attendant lords. At the height of the fun a messenger arrives to tell her that her father, the King of France, is dead, and the whole tone changes radically. She says that she and her ladies must leave; but, before they do the King and his lords apologise for their extreme behaviour. Then the King expresses the men's real feelings by asking her and her ladies to 'Grant us your loves' on behalf of himself and his lords. This is her response to their over-apologies and to their proposals, which the ladies had previously only regarded as 'courtship, pleasant jest, and courtesy'. She could be as young as late teens.

----

1   *perjured* maligned by himself
2   *dear* serious (but forgivable because it was born out of his love for her)
3   *as there is no such cause* although I can't think (why my love should prompt you to do anything)
6   *naked* austere
8   *twelve celestial signs* signs of the Zodiac
12 *weeds* rough clothes
14 *last love* remain in love
16 *challenge* claim
    challenge by these deserts (In the majority of editions this is 'challenge me by these deserts' – I prefer it without the 'me'.)
    by these deserts in reward for your penance
17 *palm now kissing thine* (she presses the palm of her hand to his)
18 *instance* (This is 'instant' in some editions.)

Act 5, Scene 2
Princess –

1   No, no, my lord, your grace is perjured much,
        Full of dear guiltiness, and therefore this:
        If for my love – as there is no such cause –
        You will do aught, this shall you do for me:
5   Your oath I will not trust; but go with speed
        To some forlorn and naked hermitage,
        Remote from all the pleasures of the world.
        There stay until the twelve celestial signs
        Have brought about the annual reckoning.
10   If this austere, insociable life
        Change not your offer made in heat of blood;
        If frosts and fasts, hard lodging and thin weeds
        Nip not the gaudy blossoms of your love,
        But that it bear this trial, and last love;
15   Then at the expiration of the year
        Come challenge me, challenge by these deserts;
        And, by this virgin palm now kissing thine,
        I will be thine; and, till that instance, shut
        My woeful self up in a mourning house,
20   Raining the tears of lamentation
        For the remembrance of my father's death.
        If this thou do deny, let our hands part;
23   Neither entitled in the other's heart.

Love's Labour's Lost

Rosaline

Rosaline is one of the three ladies-in-waiting to the Princess of France when she visits the court of Navarre (then an independent state, but now part in Spain and part in France). Rosaline is a witty, charming and assertive young lady who is attracted by Berowne, one of the three lords attending the King of Navarre. In the male-female battle of wits that is the main theme of the play, the women come out on top. The men have just confessed their real feelings for the ladies, and the other ladies have told their individual men what they must do to prove their loves. Rosaline is the last to speak – to Berowne, the leading hedonist of the men. She is telling him that he must devote a year to more productive pursuits before she will consider marrying him. She could be as young as late teens.

She has a lot of similarities with Beatrice in *Much Ado About Nothing*, Portia in *Merchant of Venice* and Rosalind (with a 'd') in *As You Like It*.

----

1 *Berowne* (He is called 'Biron' in some editions; generally pronounce 'Be' (as in 'Ben') – 'roan'.)
4 *comparisons* ('scornful' is implied)
   flouts jibes
5 *all estates* all sorts of people
7 *wormwood* (literally a bitter-tasting herb, but here used figuratively to mean malice)
11 *still* always
13 *fierce* passionate
14 *the painèd impotent* those crippled by pain
13 *dear* heartfelt
20 *that fault withal* in spite of all your faults

Act 5, Scene 2
Rosaline –

1   Oft have I heard of you, my lord Berowne,
        Before I saw you; and the world's large tongue
        Proclaims you for a man replete with mocks,
        Full of comparisons and wounding flouts,
5   Which you on all estates will execute
        That lie within the mercy of your wit.
        To weed this wormwood from your fruitful brain,
        And therewithal to win me, if you please,
        Without the which I am not to be won,
10   You shall this twelvemonth term from day to day
        Visit the speechless sick, and still converse
        With groaning wretches; and your task shall be
        With all the fierce endeavour of your wit
        To enforce the painèd impotent to smile.
15   A jest's prosperity lies in the ear
        Of him that hears it, never in the tongue
        Of him that makes it. Then, if sickly ears,
        Deafed with the clamours of their own dear groans,
        Will hear your idle scorns, continue then,
20   And I will have you and that fault withal.
        But if they will not, throw away that spirit,
        And I shall find you empty of that fault,
23   Right joyful of your reformation.

Measure for Measure

Mariana

Mariana is a Viennese lady who (five years before the play) had been betrothed to Angelo, but who was heartlessly deserted by him when she lost her dowry in a shipwreck. She now leads a secluded life in 'a moated grange'. Angelo is the Duke of Vienna's deputy and has been ordered to begin a crack down on immorality in the city whilst his master is away. The Duke meanwhile does not leave but disguises himself as a Friar to observe what happens. Claudio has been sentenced to death for fornication. Angelo offers to spare Claudio only if his sister Isabella sleeps with him. The Duke devises a way to save both Claudio's life and Isabella's honour: he arranges for Mariana to take Isabella's place on the night of her assignation with Angelo in the garden house. In the dark Angelo does not realise that he has been tricked. The Duke then sends a letter to Angelo saying that he is returning and wishes to be met at the gates of the city. He instructs that 'if any crave redress of justice' their complaints will be publicly heard. He arrives, and Isabella is the first to accuse Angelo, followed by Mariana.

She could be any age from early twenties to mid-thirties.

I have cut a number of other characters' lines and slightly changed one of Mariana's to construct this speech.

Just using part of this speech for audition would be perfectly acceptable, e.g. lines 13–29.

———————————

3   *known* had sex with (She uses the word in the conventional sense in the next line. Similar word-play occurs in lines 11–12.)

6   *She* (i.e. Isabella)

9   *depose* testify

10 *effect of* outward manifestation

13 *unmask* unveil. (This stage direction is after the line in some editions.)

16–7 *the hand... thine* (This is referring to the 'handfasting' ceremony of a betrothal.)

18 *match* assignation

19 *supply* satisfy

22 *sense* significance

23 *I am affianced this man's wife* (This makes it is perfectly acceptable for her to have slept with Angelo.)

28 *confixèd* firmly fixed

Act 5, Scene 1
Mariana –

1   My lord, I do confess I ne'er was married,
     And I confess besides I am no maid;
     I have known my husband, yet my husband
     Knows not that ever he knew me.
5   Now I come to 't, my lord:
     She that accuses him of fornication
     In self-same manner doth accuse my husband,
     And charges him, my lord, with such a time
     When, I'll depose, I had him in mine arms
10   With all th' effect of love – and he is Angelo,
     Who thinks he knows that he ne'er knew my body,
     But knows, he thinks, that he knows Isabel's.
     [*unveiling*] Now I will unmask.
     This is that face, thou cruel Angelo,
15   Which once thou swor'st was worth the looking on.
     This is the hand which, with a vowed contract,
     Was fast belocked in thine. This is the body
     That took away the match from Isabel,
     And did supply thee at thy garden-house
20   In her imagined person. [*kneeling before the Duke*] Noble
       prince,
     As there comes light from heaven, and words from breath,
     As there is sense in truth, and truth in virtue,
     I am affianced this man's wife, as strongly
     As words could make up vows. And, my good lord,
25   But Tuesday night last gone, in 's garden-house,
     He knew me as a wife. As this is true,
     Let me in safety raise me from my knees,
     Or else forever be confixèd here,
29   A marble monument.

The Merchant of Venice

Jessica

Jessica is the daughter of Shylock, the Jewish money-lender, and beloved of Lorenzo, a Christian. She is an apparently straightforward and lively young woman, but she abandons both her father and her religion when she elopes with Lorenzo, She also takes Shylock's money with her. In Shakespeare's time her actions would have been seen as largely justified in the prevailing anti-Semitic climate. Money-lending was strictly against the Christian ethic, so the job fell to the Jewish 'outcasts', which then served to make them hated. However, Shylock does generate some sympathy. In playing Jessica now, I think it is important to take on board (at least to some extent) the enormity of what she is actually doing – it can't entirely be a completely spontaneous decision. She is talking to Lorenzo from an upstairs window or balcony.

She is probably in her mid or late teens.

I freely admit that cutting Lorenzo's lines to create this speech is somewhat cheeky and marginally changes the sense of some lines. However, I believe it makes a very interesting speech as she hovers on the edge of going through with her plans.

----

4   *who* whom
8   *exchange* (i.e. her disguise as a boy, her desertion of Shylock and her theft of his jewellery and money)
10 *pretty follies* silly mistakes
13 *hold a candle* expose (both in her change of clothes and what she's done to her father)
14 *light* wanton (and literally that of the candle)
15 *of discovery* which brings to light
16 *obscured* hidden
17 *gild myself* cover myself (with gold)
18 *ducats* (Gold (or silver) coins worth about 50p, then; now probably equivalent to about ten pounds; the silver ones were about a third of this value)

The Merchant of Venice

Act 2, Scene 6
Jessica –

Enter Jessica above in boy's clothes
1   Who are you? Tell me for more certainty,
     Albeit I'll swear that I do know your tongue's
     Lorenzo, certain, and my love indeed,
     For who love I so much? And now who knows
5   But you, Lorenzo, whether I am yours?
     Here, catch this casket; it is worth the pains.
     I am glad 'tis night, you do not look on me,
     For I am much ashamed of my exchange;
     But love is blind, and lovers cannot see
10   The pretty follies that themselves commit;
     For if they could, Cupid himself would blush
     To see me thus transformèd to a boy.
     What, must I hold a candle to my shames?
     They in themselves, good sooth, are too too light.
15   Why, 'tis an office of discovery, love,
     And I should be obscured.
     I will make fast the doors, and gild myself
18   With some more ducats, and be with you straight. *Exit above*

The Merry Wives of Windsor

Mistress (Alice) Ford

Mistress (Alice) Ford is the Elizabethan equivalent of a bored suburban housewife, married to the neurotic Frank Ford ('the sweet woman leads an ill life'). The famously fat and debauched Sir John Falstaff, whom she hardly knows, has written her a love letter, which she seems to be insulted by, but I think she might also be slightly flattered to receive such at her age (her husband says, 'my wife is not young'). Although she is generally played in her forties, she could be as young as thirty. She immediately rushes to see her friend, Mistress (Margaret) Page. They exchange a few witty remarks and then she gets to the point.

----

1 *burn daylight* waste time
2 *knighted* (literally, gain honour, but she's punning on the fact that Falstaff is a knight)
4 *make difference of* discriminate between
  liking looks
6 *uncomeliness* improper behaviour
7 *disposition* character
  gone to gone along with
8 *adhere* go together
9 *Hundredth Psalm* ('Make a joyful noise unto the Lord, all ye lands'. Some editions have 'hundred and fifty psalms' or 'hundred Psalms'.)
10 *'Greensleeves'* (A popular love song, often associated with prostitution in Shakespeare's day, to the tune of which numerous lyrics were set. It is in 6/8 time.)
  trow wonder
11 *tuns* casks
13 *entertain him* fill his thoughts

Act 2, Scene 1
Mistress Ford –

1   We burn daylight. Here: read, read. [*She gives Mistress Page a letter*] Perceive how I might be knighted.
[*Mistress Page reads*]
I shall think the worse of fat men as long as I have an eye to make difference of men's liking. And yet he would not
5   swear; praised women's modesty; and gave such orderly and well behaved reproof to all uncomeliness that I would have sworn his disposition would have gone to the truth of his words. But they do no more adhere and keep place together than the Hundredth Psalm to the tune of
10   'Greensleeves'. What tempest, I trow, threw this whale, with so many tuns of oil in his belly, ashore at Windsor? How shall I be revenged on him? I think the best way were to entertain him with hope till the wicked fire of lust have
14   melted him in his own grease. Did you ever hear the like?

The Merry Wives of Windsor

Mistress (Margaret) Page

Mistress (Margaret) Page is the Elizabethan equivalent of a suburban housewife, happily married to the mild and cheerful George, and mother to Anne and William. She hardly knows the famously fat and debauched Sir John Falstaff ('he hath not been thrice in my company.'), but has just received a love letter from him and almost immediately encounters her friend Mistress (Alice) Ford – also with a letter. She is generally a good humoured and charming lady. Although she is generally played in her forties, she could be as young as thirty.

I have constructed this speech by cutting Mistress Ford's comments and a few words of Mistress Page's.

———————————

3   *ill opinions* (i.e. Falstaff's belief that she and Mistress Ford would be interested in him.)

4–5   *let thine inherit first* let your letter qualify you to him first (in spite of the fact that they're 'twins' and therefore equally entitled to the 'inheritance'.)

8   *out of doubt* undoubtedly

9   *press* (a) printing-press, (b) intercourse

10   *Mount Pelion* (In classical mythology the Titans, when they rebelled against the gods, sought to reach the top of Olympus (home of the gods) by piling Mount Ossa on Pelion. The gods revenged themselves by burying the Titans under the mountains they had sought to move. The fate of these ladies would be similar under Falstaff.)

11   *turtles* turtle-doves (proverbial for their fidelity)

12–13   *wrangle... honesty* behave in a way contrary to my own virtue

13   *entertain* think of

14   *withal* with

      strain tendency

15   *boarded* made advances to (she continues the nautical / sexual imagery)

16   *fury* impetuous fashion

18   *comfort* encouragement

19   *a fine-baited delay* delaying tactics full of tempting allurements

20   *Host of the Garter* (Landlord of the inn Falstaff is staying at.)

Act 2, Scene 1
Mistress Page –

1   [*Comparing the two letters*] Letter for letter, but that the
     name of Page and Ford differs. [*She gives Mistress Ford her
     letter*] To thy great comfort in this mystery of ill opinions,
     here's the twin-brother of thy letter. But let thine inherit
5   first, for I protest mine never shall. I warrant he hath a
     thousand of these letters, writ with blank space for
     different names – sure, more – and these are of the second
     edition. He will print them, out of doubt; for he cares not
     what he puts into the press when he would put us two. I
10   had rather be a giantess, and lie under Mount Pelion. Well,
     I will find you twenty lascivious turtles ere one chaste man.
     It makes me almost ready to wrangle with mine own
     honesty. I'll entertain myself like one that I am not
     acquainted withal; for, sure, unless he know some strain in
15   me that I know not myself, he would never have boarded
     me in this fury. If he come under my hatches, I'll never to
     sea again. Let's be revenged on him. Let's appoint him a
     meeting, give him a show of comfort in his suit, and lead
     him on with a fine-baited delay till he hath pawned his
20   horses to mine Host of the Garter. Why, look where he
     comes, and my good man too. He's as far from jealousy as
     I am from giving him cause; and that, I hope, is an
23   unmeasurable distance.

The Merry Wives of Windsor

Mistress Quickly

Mistress Quickly is similar to but not the same as the character of the same name in *Henry IV* and *Henry V*. In this play she is 'nurse, or his dry nurse, or his cook, or his laundry, his washer and his wringer' and unknown to Falstaff at the beginning. However, she is similarly shrewd and comic, and very happy to meddle in other people's affairs, as her counterpart in the history plays. The 'Merry Wives' have hatched a plot against Falstaff in revenge for his advances upon them. He, disguised as Herne the hunter, is persuaded that the 'wives' will meet him at an ancient sacred oak at midnight. The women duly appear, but are soon frightened off by a group of 'fairies and elves', in fact Mistress Quickly and others, who then proceed with a strange ceremony. Although she is generally played older, she could be as young as her mid-twenties.

———————————

1 *About* Get to work
3 *ouphes* elves
4 *the perpetual doom* the Day of Judgement
5 *In state as wholesome as in state 'tis fit* Sound in condition ('state') as it is fitting in dignity ('state')
6 *Worthy the owner, and the owner it.* Befitting the owner (Queen Elizabeth), and the only owner appropriate to it.
7 *chairs of order* (seats (in St. George's Chapel, Windsor) individually assigned to the knights who are members of the Order of the Garter)
   look make sure
8 *balm* sweet smelling oil
9 *instalment* place ('stall') where a knight is installed
   coat coat of arms
   sev'ral crest separate heraldic figure
10 *blazon* shield (or banner) bearing a coat of arms
12 *compass* circumference
13 *expressure* expression
15 *'Honi soit qui mal y pense'* 'Evil be to him who evil thinks' (the motto of the Order of the Garter)
16 *tufts* small bunches
19 *charactery* writing
21 *dance of custom* customary dance
22 *Herne the Hunter* (a mythological character who wears stag's antlers)

Act 5, Scene 5
Mistress Quickly –

Mistress Quickly as Queen of Fairies
1   About, about!
        Search Windsor Castle, elves, within and out.
        Strew good luck, ouphes, on every sacred room,
        That it may stand till the perpetual doom
5   In state as wholesome as in state 'tis fit,
        Worthy the owner, and the owner it.
        The several chairs of order look you scour
        With juice of balm and every precious flower.
        Each fair instalment, coat, and sev'ral crest
10   With loyal blazon evermore be blessed!
        And nightly, meadow-fairies, look you sing,
        Like to the Garter's compass, in a ring.
        Th' expressure that it bears, green let it be,
        More fertile-fresh than all the field to see;
15   And *'Honi soit qui mal y pense'* write
        In em'rald tufts, flowers purple, blue, and white,
        Like sapphire, pearl, and rich embroidery,
        Buckled below fair knighthood's bending knee:
        Fairies use flowers for their charactery.
20   Away, disperse! – But till 'tis one o'clock
        Our dance of custom, round about the oak
22 .   Of Herne the hunter, let us not forget.

Much Ado About Nothing

Hero

Hero is the daughter of Leonato, the governor of Messina. On the surface she is a well brought up young lady. However, she is perfectly capable – as in this scene – of having fun. She is with her two gentlewomen, Margaret and Ursula – who are her close friends whilst also being her servants. Everybody knows that Hero's cousin Beatrice is madly in love with Benedick (and vice-versa), but neither will admit it to the other. This is Hero setting up a ploy to trick Beatrice into following her true feelings. The stage directions say that they are in Leonato's orchard and there is a definite feeling of a carefree summer's day to the scene. She could be any age between mid-teens and early twenties.

---

1   *parlour* (In a big house like Leonato's the parlour was for family use.)
3   *Proposing* Talking together
7   *steal* come secretly
    pleachèd bower (natural shelter formed by branches intertwining)
12   *listen our propose* overhear our conversation (as line 3 above)
    office task
9–11   *like favourites... bred it* like royal favourites who turn against their masters
15   *alley* pathway
    trace walk
20   *Of this matter* In this way
22   *only wounds* wounds only
23–4   *lapwing, runs / Close by the ground* (The lapwing, or pewit, draws predators from its nest by moving through the grass in this manner.)
25   *conference* conversation

Act 3, Scene 1
Hero –

Enter Hero and her two gentlewomen, Margaret and Ursula

1 Good Margaret, run thee to the parlour.
There shalt thou find my cousin Beatrice
Proposing with the Prince and Claudio.
Whisper her ear, and tell her I and Ursula
5 Walk in the orchard, and our whole discourse
Is all of her. Say that thou overheard'st us,
And bid her into the pleachèd bower
Where honeysuckles, ripened by the sun,
Forbid the sun to enter – like favourites
10 Made proud by princes, that advance their pride
Against that power that bred it. There will she hide her
To listen our propose. This is thy office.
Bear thee well in it, and leave us alone.
Margaret assents and goes
Now, Ursula, when Beatrice doth come,
15 As we do trace this alley up and down
Our talk must only be of Benedick.
When I do name him, let it be thy part
To praise him more than ever man did merit.
My talk to thee must be how Benedick
20 Is sick in love with Beatrice. Of this matter
Is little Cupid's crafty arrow made,
That only wounds by hearsay. [*Enter Beatrice, secretively*]
   Now begin,
For look where Beatrice, like a lapwing, runs
24 Close by the ground to hear our conference.

Pericles

Dionyza

Dionyza is the wife of Cleon, Governor of Tarsus. Earlier in the play Pericles (thinking that his own wife, Thaisa, is dead) has left his infant daughter, Marina, in their care. As Marina grows she over-shadows Dionyza's own daughter. The jealous foster-mother forces her servant Leonine to swear to kill Marina. Dionyza could be any age between late twenties and mid-forties.

Pericles is a play for which we have no 'authentic' text and there is much dispute amongst academics on many of the details. The above is my own version based on five different editions.

---

3   *soon* easily

6   *Enslave* (This is 'Inflame' in some editions.)

     too nicely excessively

8–9 (This stage direction is between lines 10 and 11 in some editions.)

9   *only* dear

11   *keep alone* keep to yourself

12   *How chance* How is it

14   *Have you a nurse of me!* Take me as your nurse!

      favour's beauty is

16   *On the sea-margent* At the edge (margin) of the sea

17   *quick* invigorating

18   *pierces and sharpens the stomach* penetrates (and does good) to the digestive system and increases the appetite

Pericles

Act 4, Scene 1 (Scene 15 in some versions)
Dionyza –

Tarsus, near the sea-shore. Enter Dionyza with Leonine.
1   Thy oath remember; thou hast sworn to do 't.
    'Tis but a blow, which never shall be known.
    Thou canst not do a thing i' th' world so soon,
    To yield thee so much profit. Let not conscience,
5   Which is but cold, or flaming love thy bosom
    Enslave too nicely; nor let pity, which
    Even women have cast off, melt thee; but be
    A soldier to thy purpose.
Enter Marina with a basket of flowers.
She approaches the tomb of her nurse, Lychordia.
    Here she comes weeping for her only nurse's death.
10 Thou art resolved?
    How now, Marina, why do you keep alone?
    How chance my daughter is not with you?
    Do not consume your blood with sorrowing:
    Have you a nurse of me! Lord, how your favour's
15 Changed with this unprofitable woe!
    Come, give me your flowers. On the sea-margent
    Walk with Leonine; the air is quick there,
    And it pierces and sharpens the stomach.
19 Come, Leonine, take her by the arm, walk with her.

Pericles

Dionyza

Dionyza is the wife of Cleon, Governor of Tarsus. Earlier in the play Pericles (thinking that his own wife, Thaisa, is dead) has left his infant daughter, Marina, in their care. As Marina grows she over-shadows Dionyza's own daughter. The jealous foster-mother forces her servant Leonine to swear to kill Marina, and when she believes that he's done it, kills him. At this point Cleon has just found out and his conscience is deeply troubled. Dionyza is trying to put 'fire in his belly'. She has to ensure that he will connive with her in telling Pericles that his daughter died of 'natural causes'. (There are similarities with the relationship between Macbeth and his wife.) Dionyza could be any age between late twenties and mid-forties.

Pericles is a play for which we have no 'authentic' text and there is much dispute amongst academics on many of the details. The above is my own version based on five different editions.

In the play this is not a continuous speech – sections are taken from different parts of the scene.

-----

4   *She did distain my child* She overshadowed my child (by making her seem uninteresting)
7   *blurted at* treated contemptuously (To 'blurt' is to make a derisive snorting noise.)
    mawkin slut (often spelt 'malkin')
10 *You not your child well loving* You who doesn't love your own child properly
11 *greets* pleases
    kindness natural affection
15 *yet* still
18 *care in us* great care taken by us
21 *winter kills the flies* (i.e. the obvious is true – in an attempt to appear credible. Something like a politician proclaiming that 'Knives are dangerous' – without any qualification; sounds good but means nothing.)

Act 4, Scene 3 (Scene 17 in some versions)
Dionyza –

Enter Cleon and Dionyza in mourning garments

1   Why are you foolish? Can it be undone?
Yet none does know but you how she came dead,
Nor none can know, Leonine being gone.
She did distain my child, and stood between
5   Her and her fortunes. None would look on her,
But cast their gazes on Marina's face,
Whilst ours was blurted at, and held a mawkin,
Not worth the time of day. It pierced me through.
And though you call my course unnatural,
10   You not your child well loving, yet I find
It greets me as an enterprise of kindness
Performed to your sole daughter.
And as for Pericles,
What should he say? We wept after her hearse,
15   And yet we mourn. Her monument
Is almost finished, and her epitaphs
In glittering golden characters express
A general praise to her, and care in us
At whose expense 'tis done.
20   Ye are like one that superstitiously
Doth swear to th' gods that winter kills the flies;
22   But yet I know you'll do as I advise.   *Exeunt*

Richard II

Duchess of Gloucester, Eleanor de Bohun

The Duchess of Gloucester, Eleanor de Bohun (1367–1399) was the widow of Duke Thomas of Gloucester, who was murdered in 1397 – thus historically she would be about 30 at this point. Many people regard Shakespeare's Duchess as being a similar age to her brother-in-law Gaunt (who was 57 at the time), but I don't see why she can't be played at her historical age. The only argument that I can see for her being Gaunt's contemporary is the fact that she seems very familiar with him, i.e. calling him 'Old Gaunt'; and never using his title. However, this is her only scene and this over-familiarity could be simply down to a mutual fondness; her husband Duke Thomas was the 'baby of the family' and, I suggest, he and his wife could invite such affection.

She thinks that Richard II ordered her husband's recent murder and urges Gaunt to take vengeance on him. Gaunt (in the play, a man of 'old-fashioned' chivalric values) insists that vengeance against a King can only be taken by God. This is her response.

———————————

1   *brotherhood* (Her murdered husband was Gaunt's younger brother.)
3   *Edward* (Edward III, father of Gaunt and of her husband (and five other sons). He was also something of a hero-King and reigned for 50 years – a record not surpassed until George III nearly 600 years later.)
6   *dried by nature's course* died naturally (in infancy, very common at that time)
7   *by the destinies cut* reached maturity but died (in battle or from disease)
13   *envy* hatred
15   *mettle* courage or excellence
     self same
17   *consent* acquiesce to
19   *wretched* unfortunate
20   *model* copy (also implying 'as great as')
22   *suff'ring* allowing
23   *the naked pathway to thy life* how easily your own life could also be threatened
25   *mean men* ordinary men (as opposed to the nobility)
28   *venge* avenge

Richard II

Act 1, Scene 2
Duchess of Gloucester –

> *Enter John of Gaunt, Duke of Lancaster, with the*
> *Duchess of Gloucester*

1   Finds brotherhood in thee no sharper spur?
     Hath love in thy old blood no living fire?
     Edward's seven sons, whereof thyself art one,
     Were as seven vials of his sacred blood,
5   Or seven fair branches springing from one root.
     Some of those seven are dried by nature's course,
     Some of those branches by the destinies cut;
     But Thomas, my dear lord, my life, my Gloucester,
     One vial full of Edward's sacred blood,
10   One flourishing branch of his most royal root,
     Is cracked, and all the precious liquor spilt;
     Is hacked down, and his summer leaves all faded
     By envy's hand and murder's bloody axe.
     Ah, Gaunt, his blood was thine! That bed, that womb,
15   That mettle, that self mould that fashioned thee,
     Made him a man; and though thou liv'st and breathest,
     Yet art thou slain in him. Thou dost consent
     In some large measure to thy father's death
     In that thou seest thy wretched brother die,
20   Who was the model of thy father's life.
     Call it not patience, Gaunt, it is despair.
     In suff'ring thus thy brother to be slaught'red
     Thou show'st the naked pathway to thy life,
     Teaching stern murder how to butcher thee.
25   That which in mean men we entitle patience
     Is pale cold cowardice in noble breasts.
     What shall I say? To safeguard thine own life
28   The best way is to venge my Gloucester's death.

Richard II

Duchess of Gloucester, Eleanor de Bohun

The Duchess of Gloucester, Eleanor de Bohun (1367–1399) was the widow of Duke Thomas of Gloucester, who was murdered in 1397 – thus historically she would be about 30 at this point. Many people regard Shakespeare's Duchess as being a similar age to her brother-in-law Gaunt (who was 57 at the time), but I don't see why she can't be played at her historical age. The only argument that I can see for her being Gaunt's contemporary is the fact that she seems very familiar with him, i.e. calling him 'Old Gaunt'; and never using his title. However, this is her only scene and this over-familiarity could be simply down to a mutual fondness; her husband Duke Thomas was the 'baby of the family' and, I suggest, he and his wife could invite such affection.

She thinks that Richard II ordered her husband's recent murder and urges Gaunt to take vengeance on him. Gaunt (in the play, a man of 'old-fashioned' chivalric values) insists that vengeance against a King can only be taken by God. She has just been (kindly) rebuffed again by Gaunt, but she will not give up.

---

3   *Our cousin Hereford* (Henry Bolingbroke, Duke of Hereford (later Henry IV); Gaunt's son and the Duchess's nephew. The word 'cousin' was often used for any 'relative'.)

　　fell deeply unpleasant (that's an understatement)

　　Mowbray (Thomas Mowbray, Duke of Norfolk, the man whom Hereford has accused of killing her husband, and other crimes. In Scene 1, Mowbray denies the charges and insists on trial by combat, which is arranged for Coventry.)

6   *if misfortune miss the first career* if misfortune does not overcome (Mowbray) at the first encounter (To 'career' a horse was to run it at full speed and then stop suddenly in a joust. In the following lines she imagines Mowbray overbalancing at the stop and being 'thrown'.)

10   *caitiff, recreant* base wretch, traitorous. (There is no comma in some editions.)

11   *sometimes* dead

12–13   (Gaunt has two lines here, about going to Coventry and wishing her well, which only provoke her to a further outpouring. I think he is also trying to leave at lines 18 and 19.)

13–14   *Grief boundeth... but weight* (My) grief continues to bounce ('bound', as in leap) like a ball, because of its weight (i.e. the grief's), not because of its 'hollowness' (i.e. lack of sincerity).

17 & 22   *Edmund York* (another son of Edward III, the brother in between Gaunt and her dead husband)

21   *Pleshey* (Gloucester's country house, near Dunmow in Essex. This is spelt 'Plashy' in some editions.)

23   *unfurnished walls* (before plaster and wallpaper the stone walls of the grander houses (and castles) would be hung with tapestries to brighten them up and help with insulation)

24   *Unpeopled offices* Completely devoid of the servants (she would normally expect)

Act 1, Scene 2
Duchess of Gloucester –

1   Farewell, old Gaunt.
      Thou goest to Coventry, there to behold
      Our cousin Hereford and fell Mowbray fight.
      O, set my husband's wrongs on Hereford's spear,
5   That it may enter butcher Mowbray's breast!
      Or if misfortune miss the first career,
      Be Mowbray's sins so heavy in his bosom
      That they may break his foaming courser's back
      And throw the rider headlong in the lists,
10   A caitiff, recreant to my cousin Hereford!
      Farewell, old Gaunt. Thy sometimes brother's wife
      With her companion, grief, must end her life.
      Yet one word more. Grief boundeth where it falls,
      Not with the empty hollowness, but weight.
15   I take my leave before I have begun,
      For sorrow ends not when it seemeth done.
      Commend me to thy brother, Edmund York.
      Lo, this is all – nay, yet depart not so!
      Though this be all, do not so quickly go.
20   I shall remember more. Bid him – ah, what? –
      With all good speed at Pleshey visit me.
      Alack, and what shall good old York there see
      But empty lodgings and unfurnished walls,
      Unpeopled offices, untrodden stones,
25   And what hear there for welcome but my groans?
      Therefore commend me; let him not come there
      To seek out sorrow that dwells everywhere.
      Desolate, desolate will I hence and die.
29   The last leave of thee takes my weeping eye.   *Exeunt*

Richard II

Queen Isabel

Queen Isabel was the wife of King Richard II. In reality she was a child at the time of these events, however, Shakespeare gives her the maturity of someone at least in her early twenties. Although we only actually see them briefly together in the first scene, it seems to be a very loving relationship. In many ways she is the 'human interest' (in amongst all the politics) of the play.

Richard was one of those sometimes strong and good and sometimes weak and corrupt rulers – he was unlucky to be King at a time of economic crisis. After numerous 'ups and downs' he was eventually forced to abdicate (and subsequently murdered) by his cousin Henry Bolingbroke who then became King Henry IV. At this point Richard has just abdicated and is being taken to the Tower of London.

I have cut a speech of Richard's between lines 15 and 16 in which he encourages her to give in, this only makes her want him to fight back.

---

2   *Julius Caesar's ill-erected Tower* the Tower of London (There was a legend that it had originally been built by Julius Caesar.)

     ill-erected built for evil purposes (She is especially thinking of its immediate use of imprisoning Richard.)

3   *flint* merciless (and literally built of 'flint')

7–10 (She is speaking to herself, ignoring her ladies, as she sees Richard in his piteous state.)

8   *rose* (Richard was 'rose-like' to a number of people.)

9   *you* (i.e. Isabel herself)

9–10 *That you in pity... true-love tears* Show how much you love him (through tears) and consequently give him the strength to overcome his situation

11 (Richard is now close enough for her to speak to directly.)

     the model where old Troy did stand (She is comparing his present state to that of the ruins of the once great city.)

     old Troy (London was known as 'new Troy', because of a legend that after the Trojan war a party of Trojans came to Britain and founded London.)

12 *map of honour* shadow of former glory (something on a map is very different in reality)

13–15 *inn / alehouse* (The former (Richard) is much more up-market than the latter (Bolingbroke).)

21 *To be* At being

22 *kiss the rod* give in meekly to punishment (with a 'rod')

24 *Which art* You who are

Act 5, Scene 1
Queen Isabel –

A street leading to the Tower of London.
Enter the Queen, with her attendant Ladies
1 This way the King will come. This is the way
To Julius Caesar's ill-erected Tower,
To whose flint bosom my condemnèd lord
Is doomed a prisoner by proud Bolingbroke.
5 Here let us rest, if this rebellious earth
Have any resting for her true King's Queen.
Enter Richard under guard
But soft, but see – or rather do not see –
My fair rose wither. Yet look up, behold,
That you in pity may dissolve to dew,
10 And wash him fresh again with true-love tears.
Ah, thou the model where old Troy did stand!
Thou map of honour, thou King Richard's tomb,
And not King Richard! Thou most beauteous inn:
Why should hard-favoured grief be lodged in thee,
15 When triumph is become an alehouse guest?
What, is my Richard both in shape and mind
Transformed and weakenèd? Hath Bolingbroke
Deposed thine intellect? Hath he been in thy heart?
The lion dying thrusteth forth his paw
20 And wounds the earth, if nothing else, with rage
To be o'erpowered. And wilt thou, pupil-like,
Take the correction mildly, kiss the rod,
And fawn on rage with base humility,
24 Which art a lion and the King of beasts?

Richard II

Duchess of York, Isabel of Castile

The Duchess of York, Isabel of Castile (1355–1393) was wife to Edmund Langley, Duke of York and uncle to King Richard II. Richard II has just been deposed by Henry Bolingbroke (Richard's cousin and York's nephew, who becomes King Henry IV) and the Duke has asserted his loyalty to the new King, in spite of previously supporting Richard. The York's son, the Duke of Aumerle, appears and they discover that he is involved in a plot against the new King. The Duke immediately decides to set off to warn Bolingbroke determined to alleviate the stain on his family's honour ('Bring me my boots. I will unto the King'). The Duchess pleads with him not to give their son away. She would have been in her forties at this point but could be played younger.

This speech is constructed from two shorter ones and I have modified the lineation (lines 8–9), which corresponds to that in the New Penguin edition.

----

2   *trespass of thine own* treason of your own (son)
4   *my teeming-date* the time during which I was able have children
8   *groaned* (through the process of childbirth)

Act 5, Scene 2
Duchess of York –

1   Why, York, what wilt thou do?
      Wilt thou not hide the trespass of thine own?
      Have we more sons? Or are we like to have?
      Is not my teeming-date drunk up with time?
5   And wilt thou pluck my fair son from mine age,
      And rob me of a happy mother's name?
      Is he not like thee? Is he not thine own?
      Hadst thou groaned for him as I have done
      Thou wouldst be more pitiful.
10   But now I know thy mind: thou dost suspect
      That I have been disloyal to thy bed,
      And that he is a bastard, not thy son.
      Sweet York, sweet husband, be not of that mind.
      He is as like thee as a man may be;
15   Not like to me, or any of my kin,
      And yet I love him.

Richard II

Duchess of York, Isabel of Castile

The Duchess of York, Isabel of Castile (1355–1393) was wife to Edmund Langley, Duke of York and uncle to King Richard. In the play Richard II has not long been deposed by Henry Bolingbroke (Henry IV, also his nephew). The Duke has asserted his loyalty to the new King, in spite of previously supporting Richard, but then their son, Rutland (formerly the Duke of Aumerle), is discovered to be involved in a plot against the new King. The Duke immediately sets off to warn Bolingbroke determined to alleviate the stain on his family's honour. The Duchess tries to persuade him otherwise, but he is adamant; she then tells her son to try and get to the King before his father and plead for mercy. Aumerle arrives first, then York and finally the Duchess, who launches into this speech. She would have been in her forties at this point but could be played younger.

This speech is constructed from several shorter ones.

-----

1   *this hard-hearted man* (i.e. her husband)
2   *Love loving not itself, none other can* If he cannot love his own son ('Love itself'), how can her love (or be trusted) by anyone else (especially you)
3   [*Kneels*] (This stage direction is at the start of the speech in some editions; I think it works better here.)
4   *walk upon my knees* (a traditional form of proof of repentance for a sin. This is 'kneel' in some editions.)
7   *Rutland* (her son was stripped of his dukedom)
8   *Pleads he in earnest?* (i.e. her husband and in the following lines)
10 *from our breast* from my heart
11 *would be denied* wants to be refused
12 *all beside* with every other part of my being
14 *shall* (This is 'still' in some editions.)

Act 5, Scene 3
Duchess of York –

1   O King, believe not this hard-hearted man.
Love loving not itself, none other can.
Sweet York, be patient. – Hear me, gentle liege. [*Kneels*]
Forever will I walk upon my knees,

5   And never see day that the happy sees,
Till thou give joy – until thou bid me joy
By pardoning Rutland, my transgressing boy.
Pleads he in earnest? Look upon his face.
His eyes do drop no tears, his prayers are in jest.

10   His words come from his mouth; ours from our breast.
He prays but faintly, and would be denied;
We pray with heart and soul, and all beside.
His weary joints would gladly rise, I know;
Our knees shall kneel till to the ground they grow.

15   His prayers are full of false hypocrisy;
Ours of true zeal and deep integrity.
Our prayers do outpray his – then let them have

18   That mercy which true prayer ought to have.

Richard III

Queen Elizabeth

Queen Elizabeth (formerly Lady Gray, Elizabeth Woodville; 1437(?)–1492) was the first commoner to become Queen of England. She married Edward IV (successor to Henry VI) after the death of her first husband at the battle of St. Albans. She is a pawn in the troubled politics of the time. She has just heard that the King, her husband, is dead; and she enters to find her mother-in-law (the Duchess of York) and other family members. Historically, Edward IV died in 1483 when she was in her mid-forties.

She also appears in Henry VI, part 3.

I have made some minor changes to get round the fact that this speech is edited from dialogue.

---

    with her hair about her ears (This was a common demonstration of grief; Ladies would normally wear their hair up.)

2   *chide* strongly rebuke

3–4 (Essentially she is threatening suicide.)

5   *mark* (This is 'make' in some editions, with the sense, 'bring about', which changes the sense of the line.)

7   *grow the branches when the root* (the 'root' is the dead Edward, the 'branches' are the surviving family)

8   *wither not the leaves that want their sap* (as the previous line)

9   *be brief* be quick about it

15   *springs* (i.e. of water, in order to provide the tears to 'drown the world')

     reduce bring back

16   *governed by the wat'ry moon* (in astrology the moon is both feminine and queenly and it was (then) well known that the moon governed the tides)

Act 2, Scene 2
Queen Elizabeth –

Enter Queen Elizabeth with her hair about her ears

1   Ah, who shall hinder me to wail and weep,
     To chide my fortune, and torment myself?
     I'll join with black despair against my soul,
     And to myself become an enemy.
5   Ah, mark an act of tragic violence:
     Edward, my lord, thy son, our King, is dead.
     Why grow the branches when the root is gone?
     Why wither not the leaves that want their sap?
     If you will live, lament; if die, be brief,
10 That our swift-wingèd souls may catch the King's,
     Or like obedient subjects follow him
     To his new kingdom of ne'er-changing night.
     Give me no help in lamentation:
     I am not barren to bring forth complaints.
15 All springs reduce their currents to mine eyes,
     That I, being governed by the wat'ry moon,
     May send forth plenteous tears to drown the world.
     Ah, for my husband, for my dear Lord Edward!
     What stay had I but Edward, and he's gone?
20 Was never widow had so dear a loss!

Richard III

Duchess of York, Cicely Neville

The Duchess of York, Cicely Neville (1415–1495) was the mother of
Richard III. He was the youngest of her four sons, the eldest being
Edward IV, who has recently died and Richard has accelerated his grip
on power. She (and her daughter-in-law, Edward's widow Elizabeth)
have just learned that Richard has had the princes (Edward and
Elizabeth's children) murdered in the Tower. Suddenly Richard himself
appears, the women confront him with his misdeeds; he orders his
drummers and trumpeters to drown them out. The Duchess insists on
having her say. She was in her late sixties at the time, but could be
played younger.

Throughout the play she is a strong and sympathetic lady;
historically we know very little about her, but she did manage to live
until she was eighty (outliving Richard by ten years) – an incredible
achievement for those times.

I have cut some of her and Richard's lines to create this speech.

----

8   *frightful* frightening
9   *prime of manhood* early manhood
10 *age confirmed* settled maturity
12 *comfortable* cheerful
20 *complete armour* full body armour
21 *adverse party* other side
23 *Whisper* Whisper to
26 *attend* wait for

Richard III

Act 4, Scene 4
Duchess of York –

1   O let me speak!
I will be mild and gentle in my words.
Art thou so hasty? I have stayed for thee,
God knows, in torment and in agony.
5   Thou cam'st on earth to make the earth my hell.
A grievous burden was thy birth to me;
Tetchy and wayward was thy infancy;
Thy schooldays frightful, desp'rate, wild, and furious;
Thy prime of manhood daring, bold, and venturous;
10   Thy age confirmed, proud, subtle, sly, and bloody;
More mild, but yet more harmful – kind in hatred.
What comfortable hour canst thou name
That ever graced me in thy company?
Either thou wilt die by God's just ordinance
15   Ere from this war thou turn a conqueror,
Or I with grief and extreme age shall perish,
And never more behold thy face again.
Therefore take with thee my most heavy curse,
Which in the day of battle tire thee more
20   Than all the complete armour that thou wear'st.
My prayers on the adverse party fight,
And there the little souls of Edward's children
Whisper the spirits of thine enemies,
And promise them success and victory.
25   Bloody thou art, bloody will be thy end;
Shame serves thy life, and doth thy death attend.   *Exit*

Romeo and Juliet

Lady Capulet

Lady Capulet is Juliet's mother. She seems to be a staid and conventional lady, who, here, is very keen for her daughter to marry a presentable (and wealthy) young man. Previously, her husband has told Paris that Juliet is too young, at fourteen, for marriage. Between then and this scene they have obviously talked (which we don't see) and it's possible that they decide that Lady Capulet should 'test the waters'. Or she could have persuaded Capulet that Paris was too good to miss as a son -in-law – you have to make up your own mind.

After some banter with the Nurse over Juliet's age, Lady Capulet seizes a cue from the Nurse to introduce the idea of marriage with her daughter.

In lines 5–7, she heavily implies that she is 28 (given that her daughter is fourteen). However, she later refers to her 'old age', but this is at the point of discovery of her daughter's corpse. Again it is down to you to decide and be prepared to justify your decisions.

A brief (guarded) response from Juliet and the Nurse's interjections have been cut to construct this speech.

Juliet hasn't even met Romeo yet.

13–24 (Her comparison of Paris with a beautifully bound book (*volume, writ, pen, content, margent, book, unbound, cover, clasps,* story) continues over these lines.)

15 *married* harmoniously joined (also a deliberate use of the word in her attempts to persuade Juliet)
   lineament distinctive feature

16 *content* (literally, the 'contents' of the book; but she also implies 'satisfaction')

18 *written in the margent* (In sixteenth-century books the notes (the equivalent of modern footnotes) were usually printed in the margins.)

19 *unbound lover* (She likens Paris to a book without its binding (hard-cover); also, he is not yet 'bound' in marriage. There also might be sexual connotations in this, but would such a 'conventional' lady think such thoughts?)

20 *cover* (a) 'cover' of a book, (b) the loving ('covering') embraces of a wife

21–22 *The fish lives in the sea, and 'tis much pride / For fair without the fair within to hide.* It is a good and natural thing to bind a book with very good contents (Paris) with a cover (Juliet) worthy of them. A book, so bound, is in its natural surrounding – as is a fish in the sea.

21 *'tis much pride* it's good (and natural)

22 *fair without the fair within* 'fair' (cover / Juliet) outside the 'fair' (contents / Paris)
   within to hide (this refers both to the 'fish' in the 'sea' and to the 'book' within its 'cover')

23–24 *That book in many's eyes doth share the glory, / That in gold clasps locks in the golden story.* There is a 'quality' book which is esteemed by many, both for its good contents (*golden story*) and for its rich binding (*gold clasps*). As the binding and the contents share equally in the *glory*, so will you and Paris share equally in esteem when you are united in marriage. (She could also be suggesting financial advantage in the marriage by her allusions to 'gold' (and 'golden') and 'all that he doth possess'.)

24 *clasps* (a) the fastenings of the book-covers, (b) loving embraces

Act 1, Scene 3
Lady Capulet –

1   Tell me, daughter Juliet,
      How stands your dispositions to be married?
      Well, think of marriage now. Younger than you,
      Here in Verona, ladies of esteem
5   Are made already mothers. By my count
      I was your mother much upon these years
      That you are now a maid. Thus then, in brief:
      The valiant Paris seeks you for his love.
10   Verona's summer hath not such a flower.
      What say you? Can you love the gentleman?
      This night you shall behold him at our feast.
      Read o'er the volume of young Paris' face,
      And find delight writ there with beauty's pen.
15   Examine every married lineament,
      And see how one another lends content;
      And what obscured in this fair volume lies
      Find written in the margent of his eyes.
      This precious book of love, this unbound lover,
20   To beautify him only lacks a cover.
      The fish lives in the sea, and 'tis much pride
      For fair without the fair within to hide.
      That book in many's eyes doth share the glory,
      That in gold clasps locks in the golden story.
25   So shall you share all that he doth possess,
      By having him, making yourself no less.

The Tempest

Ariel

Ariel is an airy sprite – invisible to all but the magician, Prospero, who rules the island (the setting of the play) and controls everybody and everything on it. Ariel's chief job is to carry out Prospero's wishes and is here describing how she (or 'he' or 'it') contrived the wreck of the ship containing Prospero's enemies whilst ensuring that no-one was harmed.

Ariel obviously enjoys this work – indeed, Prospero is very aware that in having all this fun Ariel might go too far in the heat of the moment. Ariel's moods go up and down quite violently – a bit like a child's. The success of this mission brings a high which switches to a violent low shortly after this when Prospero says that there's more to do before her (or 'his' or 'its') promised freedom. Ariel, the magical being, has very human feelings.

Ariel can be played by either a man or a woman.

This speech is constructed from three shorter ones. It is also quite long and you could finish it at '... devils are here' (line18) or '... this sad knot.' (line 25), but I've seen the whole speech done very excitingly and it certainly didn't feel too long.

---

1   *beak* prow (think of a bird's beak leading the way)

2   *waist* amidships (the fattest section of an Elizabethan ship)

5   *boresprit* bowsprit (Some editions have 'bowsprit', but I prefer *boresprit* as it gives a great feel for a ship boring through the waves.)

   flame distinctly make myself distinct flames in these different places

6–8 *Jove's lightnings... were not.* God's lightning-bolts, that precede the great claps of thunder, weren't as good as my efforts. (Some editors prefer *lightning* (singular) but I prefer the plural as it gives the idea of multiple flashes.)

16   *up-staring* standing on end

19   *sustaining garments* (There was a belief that clothes could keep you buoyant in water – probably born out of incidences of air getting trapped by certain clothing materials, thus – like a balloon – creating some buoyancy. Or perhaps Ariel is saying that even their clothes were left undamaged, as well as their bodies. You have to make up your own mind.)

25   *this sad knot* all miserable and huddled up (possibly imitated by Ariel)

28   *still-vexed Bermoothes* (Bermoothes (the 'es' is pronounced: 'ez') is roughly the Spanish for Bermudas, which were first colonised around the time *The Tempest* was written. These islands have a very stormy climate – hence 'still-vexed'.)

30   *charm.... suffered labour* spell to calm them after the hell they just been through (probably all part of what Prospero told him to do)

33   *flote* sea

35   *wracked* wrecked (Some editors have 'wrecked', but I prefer the 'a' – it's more evocative of the state of the ship and those in it.)

Act 1, Scene 2
Ariel –

1   I boarded the King's ship. Now on the beak,
       Now in the waist, the deck, in every cabin
       I flamed amazement. Sometimes I'd divide,
       And burn in many places. On the topmast,
5   The yards, and boresprit would I flame distinctly,
       Then meet and join. Jove's lightnings, the precursors
       O' th' dreadful thunderclaps, more momentary
       And sight-outrunning were not. The fire and cracks
       Of sulphurous roaring the most mighty Neptune
10   Seem to besiege, and make his bold waves tremble,
       Yea his dread trident shake. Not a soul
       But felt a fever of the mad, and played
       Some tricks of desperation. All but mariners
       Plunged in the foaming brine, and quit the vessel,
15   Then all afire with me. The King's son Ferdinand,
       With hair up-staring – then like reeds not hair –
       Was the first man that leaped; cried, 'Hell is empty,
       And all the devils are here!' Not a hair perished.
       On their sustaining garments not a blemish,
20   But fresher than before; and as thou bad'st me,
       In troops I have dispersed them 'bout the isle.
       The King's son have I landed by himself,
       Whom I left cooling of the air with sighs
       In an odd angle of the isle, and sitting,
25   His arms in this sad knot. Safely in harbour
       Is the King's ship, in the deep nook where once
       Thou called'st me up at midnight to fetch dew
       From the still-vexed Bermoothes, there she's hid;
       The mariners all under hatches stowed,
30   Who, with a charm joined to their suffered labour,
       I have left asleep. And for the rest o' th' fleet,
       Which I dispersed, they have all met again,
       And are upon the Mediterranean flote
       Bound sadly home for Naples,
35   Supposing that they saw the King's ship wracked,
       And his great person perish.

Titus Andronicus

Tamora

Tamora, Queen of the Goths and her three sons have been captured by
Titus Andronicus, a Roman general. They have just arrived in Rome.
One of Titus' surviving sons suggests that one of Tamora's sons should
be sacrificed to appease the 'groaning shadows' of Titus' own sons killed
in the war against the Goths. Titus agrees that the eldest should be taken.
This is her final appeal to her conqueror to spare her son's life. She could
be as young as thirty.

---

3 *passion* suffering
11 *commonweal* general good of the community
12 *piety* devotion
16 *tomb* family tomb
14 *nature of the gods* (i.e. that the gods are merciful)

Act 1, Scene 1
Tamora –

1   [*Kneeling*] Stay, Roman brethren! Gracious conqueror,
Victorious Titus, rue the tears I shed,
A mother's tears in passion for her son;
And if thy sons were ever dear to thee,
5   O, think my son to be as dear to me.
Sufficeth not that we are brought to Rome
To beautify thy triumphs, and return
Captive to thee and to thy Roman yoke;
But must my sons be slaughtered in the streets
10   For valiant doings in their country's cause?
O, if to fight for King and commonweal
Were piety in thine, it is in these.
Andronicus, stain not thy tomb with blood.
Wilt thou draw near the nature of the gods?
15   Draw near them then in being merciful.
Sweet mercy is nobility's true badge;
17   Thrice-noble Titus, spare my first-born son.

Titus Andronicus

Lavinia

Lavinia is the daughter of Titus Andronicus, a Roman general, recently victorious over the Goths. He has returned to Rome with their Queen, Tamora and her three sons, the eldest of whom is sacrificed to appease the 'groaning shadows' of Titus' own sons killed in the war. Meanwhile, Saturninus, the Emperor, marries Tamora and from this secure position she begins to contemplate her revenge on Titus – with the help of her lover, Aaron. Her first targets are Lavinia and her new husband Bassanius (the Emperor's younger bother), whom Tamora and her surviving sons (Demetrius and Chiron) encounter whilst out hunting. They kill Bassanius and then begin to threaten Lavinia. She could be any age between mid-teens and early twenties.

I have cut Demetrius', Chiron's and Tamora's lines to construct this speech.

———————————

3 *learn* teach
6 *not sons alike* sons who are unlike (in temperament)
8 *find it* find it so
10 *par'd* trimmed
12 *own birds* their fledglings
14 *Nothing so kind, but something pitiful.* Not as kind as the raven, but with the potential to show pity.

Act 2, Scene 3
Lavinia –

1   Sweet lords, entreat her hear me but a word.
      When did the tiger's young ones teach the dam?
      O, do not learn her wrath! She taught it thee.
      The milk thou suck'st from her did turn to marble,
5   Even at thy teat thou hadst thy tyranny.
      Yet every mother breeds not sons alike:
      [*To Chiron*] Do thou entreat her show a woman's pity.
      Yet have I heard – O, could I find it now! –
      The lion, moved with pity, did endure
10   To have his princely paws par'd all away.
      Some say that ravens foster forlorn children
      The whilst their own birds famish in their nests.
      O, be to me, though thy hard heart say no,
      Nothing so kind, but something pitiful.
15   O, let me teach thee for my father's sake,
      That gave thee life when well he might have slain thee.
17   Be not obdurate, open thy deaf ears.

Titus Andronicus

Tamora

Tamora, Queen of the Goths was captured by Titus Andronicus, a Roman general, and brought to Rome. She has three sons, the eldest of whom is sacrificed to appease the 'groaning shadows' of Titus' own sons killed in the war against the Goths. Rather soon after, Saturninus, the Roman Emperor, marries her and from this secure position Tamora begins her contemplate her revenge on Titus – with the help of her lover, Aaron. A saga of rape, mutilation and murder follows. At this point Saturninus has just learned (from Aemilius, a Roman noble) that an army of Goths, led by Titus' son Lucius, is headed towards Rome bent on revenge. Saturninus is deeply worried because he knows that Lucius (and Titus) are more popular than he is. Tamora tries to reassure him. She could be as young as thirty.

I have cut a few lines of Saturninus' and slightly changed the words in one line.

You could just do this speech down to line 19.

----

2   *rue* regret
    like thy name (Saturn was a Roman god)
5   *Is not careful* Doesn't care
7   *at pleasure* any time he wants to
    stint stop
8   *giddy* indecisive
12 *honey-stalks* red clover (too much of which is harmful to sheep)
13 *When as* When
14 *rotted* (The 'rot' is a disease of the liver.)
16 *smooth* flatter

Act 4, Scene 4
Tamora –

1   Why should you fear? Is not your city strong?
      King, be thy thoughts imperious like thy name!
      Is the sun dimmed, that gnats do fly in it?
      The eagle suffers little birds to sing,
5   And is not careful what they mean thereby,
      Knowing that with the shadow of his wings
      He can at pleasure stint their melody.
      Even so mayst thou the giddy men of Rome.
      Then cheer thy spirit; for know thou, Emperor,
10   I will enchant the old Andronicus
      With words more sweet and yet more dangerous
      Than baits to fish or honey-stalks to sheep
      When as the one is wounded with the bait,
      The other rotted with delicious feed.
15   Tamora will entreat his son for us;
      For I can smooth and fill his agèd ears
      With golden promises that, were his heart
      Almost impregnable, his old ears deaf,
      Yet should both ear and heart obey my tongue.
20   [*To Aemilius*] Go thou before to be our ambassador:
      Say that the Emperor requests a parley
      Of warlike Lucius, and appoint the meeting
23   Even at his father's house, the old Andronicus.

Troilus And Cressida

Cressida

Cressida is the young daughter of a Trojan priest who has defected to the Greeks during the ten-year siege of Troy. She is secretly attracted to Troilus, a young Trojan prince. In this scene she has just been talking with her uncle Pandarus about individual Trojan soldiers (including Troilus) returning from the battle-field. The conversation is full of sexual innuendo. Pandarus particularly focuses her attention on Troilus, who has already expressed his interest in her to Pandarus. Cressida denies any interest in Troilus, but her uncle persists and leaves offering to return with a 'token' from him. After all the sexual banter, she starts to think more deeply about the consequences of her attraction to Troilus.

This may look like rather a short speech for audition – in fact, it's a very good length and was on a famous British drama school's list of specified options.

Different editions have Pandarus exiting before and after the first line – i.e. she can say it to herself (after he's gone (or going)) or to his face; and then he goes...

1   *bawd* pimp
3   *another's* (i.e. Troilus')
5   *glass* mirror
6   *wooing* whilst being wooed
7   *Things won are done; joy's soul lies in the doing.* To travel hopefully is better than to arrive.
8 & 10   *That she* That woman
9   *than it is* than it is worth
12   *out of love* as taught by love
13   *'Achievement is command; ungained, beseech.'* 'Once conquered, a woman is in the man's power; while she holds off, men still pursue her.'
14   *heart's content firm love doth bear* heart is full of enduring love

104

Act 1, Scene 2
Cressida –

Exit Pandarus

1   By the same token you are a bawd.
     Words, vows, gifts, tears, and love's full sacrifice
     He offers in another's enterprise;
     But more in Troilus thousand-fold I see
5   Than in the glass of Pandar's praise may be.
     Yet hold I off. Women are angels, wooing;
     Things won are done; joy's soul lies in the doing.
     That she beloved knows naught that knows not this:
     Men prize the thing ungained more than it is.
10   That she was never yet that ever knew
     Love got so sweet as when desire did sue.
     Therefore this maxim out of love I teach:
     'Achievement is command; ungained, beseech.'
     Then, though my heart's content firm love doth bear,
15   Nothing of that shall from mine eyes appear.   *Exit*

Troilus and Cressida

Cressida

Cressida is the young daughter of a Trojan priest who has defected to the Greeks during the ten-year siege of Troy. She is secretly attracted to Troilus, a young Trojan prince, but as she says earlier, 'Things won are done; joy's soul lies in the doing'. Her uncle Pandarus is aware of her secret desires; he pooh-poohs her equivocations and arranges for her to meet with Troilus – in this scene. To start with she and Troilus engage in the kind of verbal foreplay common to people desiring each other, but not quite able to commit themselves to love. Then Pandarus reappears and brings the conversation sharply back to sex. Suddenly she says openly to Troilus, 'I have loved you night and day / For many weary months'; he responds with, 'Why was my Cressid then so hard to win?'. This speech is her response.

In the play Troilus kisses her after 'Stop my mouth' (line 17), but you could add the following lines for an audition, pretending that she pulls back from that brink yet again.

---

7   *See* Stop and think
16 *in* (This is 'from' in some editions.)
17 *My soul of counsel* The secrets of my heart
    Stop my mouth. Kiss me and prevent any further self-revelation.

Act 3, Scene 2
Cressida –

1   Hard to seem won; but I was won, my lord,
       With the first glance that ever – pardon me;
       If I confess much, you will play the tyrant.
       I love you now, but till now not so much
5   But I might master it. In faith, I lie:
       My thoughts were like unbridled children, grown
       Too headstrong for their mother. See, we fools!
       Why have I blabbed? Who shall be true to us,
       When we are so unsecret to ourselves?
10   But though I loved you well, I wooed you not;
       And yet, good faith, I wished myself a man,
       Or that we women had men's privilege
       Of speaking first. Sweet, bid me hold my tongue,
       For in this rapture I shall surely speak
15   The thing I shall repent. See, see, your silence,
       Cunning in dumbness, in my weakness draws
       My soul of counsel from me. Stop my mouth.
       My lord, I do beseech you pardon me.
       'Twas not my purpose thus to beg a kiss.
20   I am ashamed. O heavens, what have I done?
21   For this time will I take my leave, my lord.

The Two Gentlemen of Verona

Silvia

Silvia is the daughter of the Duke of Milan. She is in love with Valentine and loved by both Thurio and Proteus. She and Valentine plan to elope, but they are betrayed by Proteus to her father, who banishes Valentine. She rejects Proteus' subsequent overtures and plans to seek out Valentine in Mantua (a journey of about 100 miles). She has 'entreated' Sir Eglamour to call and he asks her, 'what service it is your pleasure to command me in.' This is her response.

She is not a simpering juvenile, her dismissal of Proteus in the previous scene (for instance) shows a strong and forthright lady of some wit. We know virtually no more about Sir Eglamour than what Silvia says about him here.

----

3 *remorseful* compassionate
6 *enforce me marry* force me to marry
7 *abhors* (This is 'abhor'd' in some editions.)
11 *chastity* fidelity
12 *I would to* I want to go to
14 *for* since
16 *repose* have confidence in
17 *Urge not* Don't put forward as an excuse (for not helping me)

Act 4, Scene 3
Silvia –

1

O Eglamour, thou art a gentleman –
Think not I flatter, for I swear I do not –
Valiant, wise, remorseful, well accomplished.
Thou art not ignorant what dear good will

5   I bear unto the banished Valentine,
Nor how my father would enforce me marry
Vain Thurio, whom my very soul abhors.
Thyself hast loved, and I have heard thee say
No grief did ever come so near thy heart

10   As when thy lady and thy true love died,
Upon whose grave thou vowed'st pure chastity.
Sir Eglamour, I would to Valentine,
To Mantua, where I hear he makes abode;
And for the ways are dangerous to pass,

15   I do desire thy worthy company,
Upon whose faith and honour I repose.
Urge not my father's anger, Eglamour,
But think upon my grief, a lady's grief,
And on the justice of my flying hence,

20   To keep me from a most unholy match,
Which heaven and fortune still rewards with plagues.
I do desire thee, even from a heart
As full of sorrows as the sea of sands,
To bear me company and go with me.

25   If not, to hide what I have said to thee,
That I may venture to depart alone.

The Two Gentlemen of Verona

Silvia

Silvia is the daughter of the Duke of Milan. She is in love with Valentine and loved by both Thurio and Proteus. She and Valentine plan to elope, but they are betrayed by Proteus to her father, who banishes Valentine. She rejects Proteus' subsequent overtures and sets out to find Valentine in Mantua (a journey of about 100 miles). She is captured by outlaws; then rescued by Proteus who 'approaches' her once again. This is her response. (She knows that a lady called Julia is in love with him; what she doesn't know is that Proteus' page, who accompanies him, is in fact Julia, disguised as a boy.)

She is not a simpering juvenile, her previous dismissal of Proteus (for instance) shows a strong and forthright lady of some wit.

I have cut some of Proteus and Silvia's lines (and Julia's aside) to create this speech.

---

1   *approach* sexual advance
6   *tender* precious
14 *unless thou'dst two* unless you think it possible to be a faithful lover to both (Julia and to me)
17 *thy true friend* (i.e. Valentine)

Act 5, Scene 4
Silvia –

1 By thy approach thou mak'st me most unhappy.
  Had I been seizèd by a hungry lion
  I would have been a breakfast to the beast
  Rather than have false Proteus rescue me.
5 O heaven be judge how I love Valentine,
  Whose life's as tender to me as my soul.
  And full as much, for more there cannot be,
  I do detest false perjured Proteus.
  Therefore be gone, solicit me no more.
10 Read over Julia's heart, thy first, best love,
  For whose dear sake thou didst then rend thy faith
  Into a thousand oaths, and all those oaths
  Descended into perjury to love me.
  Thou hast no faith left now, unless thou'dst two,
15 And that's far worse than none. Better have none
  Than plural faith, which is too much by one,
17 Thou counterfeit to thy true friend.

The Two Noble Kinsmen

First Queen

The First Queen is one of three who suddenly appear to interrupt the wedding of Theseus (Duke of Athens) and Hippolyta (Queen of the Amazons). The Queens' husbands (their 'sovereigns') have been killed in an attack on Thebes (the 'Seven against Thebes'). Creon (King of Thebes) ordered that their bodies should not be buried as a warning to others who might try the same thing. The First Queen is appealing to Theseus for revenge against Creon. We know nothing more about her, so she could be almost any age you like.

The idea of a body not being buried is repulsive to us, but then it also meant that the deceased's soul would wander eternally in torment.

---

2   *who* (i.e. the 'sovereigns')
4   *foul fields* battlefields
7   *mortal loathsomeness* the rotting corpses (of the 'sovereigns')
8   *Phoebus* (Apollo, god of the sun)
10 *purger of the earth* (Theseus was famed for ridding the world of threats to civilised society.)
12 *chapel* bury (properly) in a chapel
13 *of* out of
      take some note please understand
14 *our crownèd heads* our husbands
15 *this* (i.e. the sky)
16 *vault* arched roof (i.e. the sky)

Act 1, Scene 1
First Queen –

1   [*Kneeling still*] We are three queens, whose sovereigns fell
       before
       The wrath of cruel Creon; who endured
       The beaks of ravens, talons of the kites,
       And pecks of crows in the foul fields of Thebes.
5   He will not suffer us to burn their bones,
       To urn their ashes, nor to take th' offence
       Of mortal loathsomeness from the blest eye
       Of holy Phoebus, but infects the winds
       With stench of our slain lords. O pity, Duke!
10   Thou purger of the earth, draw thy feared sword
       That does good turns to th' world; give us the bones
       Of our dead Kings, that we may chapel them;
       And of thy boundless goodness take some note
       That for our crownèd heads we have no roof,
15   Save this, which is the lion's and the bear's,
       And vault to everything.

The Two Noble Kinsmen

Emilia

Emilia is the sister of Hippolyta (Queen of the Amazons, fiancée and later the wife of the Duke of Athens, Theseus). Almost certainly this speech is Shakespeare's but because parts of the play were probably written by John Fletcher she is a somewhat confusing character. However, she is certainly a warm-hearted, sensitive young woman who is later the subject of the obsession that destroys the friendship of the 'kinsmen'. There is also the sense that Hippolyta is very much the 'big sister'.

Just before this speech, the sisters have just bade farewell to Pirithous, a close friend of Theseus'; they then both comment on how close the two men are, which leads Emilia on to talk about her childhood friend, Flavina, who died when they were both eleven.

----

2   *more ground* a firmer foundation
3   *buckled* held up
6   *I sigh and spoke of* for whom I sigh and of whom I spoke (i.e. her childhood friend, Flavinia)
7   *for* simply because
    elements (i.e. the four elements (earth, water, fire, and air) – the fundamental constituents from which everything in the universe was supposed to be made)
8–9 *effect... operance* produce amazing results (i.e. all the incredibly varied things that exist – made up from these basic 'elements') by their operation
12 *No more arraignment* Without any need for further examination (or 'accusation')
16 *like innocent cradle* (i.e. Flavinia's breasts)
    phoenix (a legendary bird, said to burn itself to ashes and then to rise again)
17 *perfume* (the fire in which the phoenix burned was made of aromatic (smelling of spice) wood)
17–18 *no toy... pattern* no trivial ornament that I didn't also wear
18 *Her affections* Whatever she took a fancy to
19 *happily her careless wear* perhaps her casual dress
20 *most serious decking* formal dress
21 *air* tune
    at adventure by chance
22 *coinage* improvisation
23 *sojourn – rather dwell on* stay with – rather, linger over
24 *rehearsal* account (of our friendship)
25 *every innocent* (This is 'seely (happy) innocence' in some editions.)
    wots knows
    comes in appears
26 *old importment's bastard* a pale ('bastard') imitation (of what it was) ('importment's' is 'emportment's' in some editions; emportment = fit of passion)
28 *in sex dividual* between people of the opposite sex

Act 1, Scene 3
Emilia –

1   You talk of Pirithous' and Theseus' love:
      Theirs has more ground, is more maturely seasoned,
      More buckled with strong judgement, and their needs
      The one of th' other may be said to water
5   Their intertangled roots of love; but I
      And she I sigh and spoke of were things innocent,
      Loved for we did, and like the elements,
      That know not what, nor why, yet do effect
      Rare issues by their operance, our souls
10   Did so to one another. What she liked
      Was then of me approved; what not, condemned –
      No more arraignment. The flower that I would pluck
      And put between my breasts – O then but beginning
      To swell about the blossom – she would long
15   Till she had such another, and commit it
      To the like innocent cradle, where, phoenix-like,
      They died in perfume. On my head no toy
      But was her pattern. Her affections – pretty,
      Though happily her careless wear – I followed
20   For my most serious decking. Had mine ear
      Stol'n some new air, or at adventure hummed one,
      From musical coinage, why, it was a note
      Whereon her spirits would sojourn – rather dwell on –
      And sing it in her slumbers. This rehearsal –
25   Which, every innocent wots well, comes in
      Like old importment's bastard – has this end:
      That the true love 'tween maid and maid may be
28   More than in sex dividual.

The Winter's Tale

Emilia

Emilia is a lady-in-waiting to Queen Hermione, who has been accused of adultery and imprisoned by her husband, King Leontes of Sicilia. Hermione is defended by Paulina (wife of one of Leontes' Lords). Here Paulina tries to visit Hermione in prison, but the goaler will only let her talk to Emilia. Paulina asks her, 'How fares our gracious lady?' This is Emilia's response.

This is Emilia's only scene and we learn no more about her, so she could be any age you like and you can supply her with any background you like.

I have made some minor changes (in words and lineation) to create this speech from three separate ones. In the play Paulina makes her 'undertaking' to help Hermione (by trying to soften the King by showing him the baby) in between lines 7 and 8, I have implied that she does this before the speech starts.

---

2 *On* Because of

5 *like to live* (It was very common then for babies to die at, or shortly after birth.)

10 *undertaking* (Paulina, in fact, makes her 'undertaking' in the speech cut from the middle of this one.)

11 *thriving issue* successful outcome

13 *presently* immediately

15 *hammered of* thought hard about

16 *tempt a minister of honour* risk asking anyone of importance

Act 2, Scene 2
Emilia –

1	She's well as one so great and so forlorn
	May hold together. On her frights and griefs –
	Which never tender lady hath borne greater –
	She is, something before her time, delivered
5	A girl; a goodly babe, lusty, like to live.
	The Queen receives much comfort in 't;
	Says, 'My poor prisoner, I am innocent as you.'
	O most worthy madam!
	Your honour and your goodness is so evident
10	That your free undertaking cannot miss
	A thriving issue. There is no lady living
	So meet for this great errand. Please your ladyship
	To visit the next room, I'll presently
	Acquaint the Queen of your most noble offer,
15	Who but today hammered of this design,
	But durst not tempt a minister of honour
17	Lest she should be denied.

The Winter's Tale

Perdita

Perdita is the long-lost daughter of King Leontes and Queen Hermione of Sicilia – not that she knows any of this until the very end of the play; she has been brought up by a simple shepherd. She is a straightforward and charming young girl in love with Florizel, son of the King of Bohemia. At this point she is 'Mistress of the Feast' at the shepherds' festival. She is sixteen.

All the flowers she mentions have symbolic connotations.

-----

3 *Mopsa and Dorcas* (Fellow shepherdesses)
5 *Proserpina* (Latin form of the Greek Persephone, wife of Pluto, King of the underworld. She was abducted by him whilst she was gathering flowers in a field.)
7 *Dis's wagon* Pluto's chariot
8 *take* enchant
9 *dim* shy (the hanging head of the violet is usually concealed or partly concealed)
10 *Juno* (the beautiful Queen of the gods)
11 *Cytherea* (Venus, the goddess of love, was called Cytherea after Cythera, the island where she first stepped ashore after her birth in the sea-foam.)
13 *Phoebus* (Apollo, the sun god)
     a malady (i.e. the green-sickness, an illness that turns the complexion to the yellowy-green colour of the primrose)
14 *incident to* common amongst
     oxlips (larger and stronger than cowslips, they stand up strongly)
15 *crown imperial* the tall, yellow fritillary
16 *flower-de-luce* fleur-de-lys (another 'regal' flower)

Act 4, Scene 4
Perdita –

1   [*To Florizel*] Now, my fair'st friend,
        I would I had some flowers o' th' spring that might
        Become your time of day – [*To Mopsa and Dorcas*] and
          yours, and yours,
        That wear upon your virgin branches yet
5   Your maidenheads growing. O Proserpina,
        For the flowers now that, frighted, thou let'st fall
        From Dis's wagon! – Daffodils,
        That come before the swallow dares, and take
        The winds of March with beauty; violets, dim,
10   But sweeter than the lids of Juno's eyes
        Or Cytherea's breath; pale primroses,
        That die unmarried ere they can behold
        Bright Phoebus in his strength – a malady
        Most incident to maids; bold oxlips, and
15   The crown imperial; lilies of all kinds,
        The flower-de-luce being one. O, these I lack,
        To make you garlands of, and my sweet friend
18   To strew him o'er and o'er.

Bibliography

The Plays

I referred to the Arden, New Penguin, Oxford, Peter Alexander and Riverside editions and found different aspects to recommend each of them. However, if I'm to recommend one particular edition – for actors – I would marginally recommend the Oxford editions. *The Complete Works* (General Editors: Stanley Wells & Gary Taylor) were published in 1988 by Oxford University Press, and about half of the individual plays have appeared in paperback with some excellent notes. The remaining plays are 'forthcoming'.

Shakespeare Reference

Charles Boyce, *Shakespeare – The Essential Reference to His Plays, His Poems, His Life, And More* (Roundtable Press)

Peter Quennell and Hamish Johnson, *Who's Who in Shakespeare* (Routledge, 1996)

Gareth and Barbara Lloyd Evans, *Everyman's Companion to Shakespeare* (Dent, 1978)

About Shakespeare and His Plays

There are an impossible number of books on this subject; the ones I've got most out of are:

Anthony Burgess, *Shakespeare* (Penguin, 1970) – this not a history book but a wonderful evocation of who Shakespeare might have been and how he might had lived his life.

A. L. Rowse, *Shakespeare the Elizabethan* (Weidenfeld & Nicholson, 1977) – although written by an eminent academic historian, this is a good read.

F. E. Halliday, *Shakespeare In His Age* (Duckworth, 1971) – a much more detailed account, involving more of the other important personalities of the age.

Jan Kott, *Shakespeare Our Contemporary* – although he writes about only a few of the plays, the author gives a wonderful evocation of Shakespeare in our time.

About Acting

Uta Hagen, *A Challenge for the Actor* (Macmillan, 1991) – the best book on acting ever written.

Simon Dunmore, *An Actor's Guide to Getting Work* (A. & C. Black, 1996) – all you need to know about auditioning and all aspects of being an actor.